T0277261

When Tobacco Was King

UNIVERSITY PRESS OF FLORIDA

Florida A&M University, Tallahassee
Florida Atlantic University, Boca Raton
Florida Gulf Coast University, Ft. Myers
Florida International University, Miami
Florida State University, Tallahassee
New College of Florida, Sarasota
University of Central Florida, Orlando
University of Florida, Gainesville
University of North Florida, Jacksonville
University of South Florida, Tampa
University of West Florida, Pensacola

When Tobacco Was King

Families, Farm Labor, and Federal Policy in the Piedmont

Evan P. Bennett

UNIVERSITY PRESS OF FLORIDA
Gainesville/Tallahassee/Tampa/Boca Raton
Pensacola/Orlando/Miami/Jacksonville/Ft. Myers/Sarasota

Copyright 2014 by Evan P. Bennett
All rights reserved
Published in the United States of America

First cloth printing, 2014
First paperback printing, 2024

29 28 27 26 25 24   6 5 4 3 2 1

Library of Congress Control Number: 2014937653
ISBN 978-0-8130-6014-9 (cloth) | ISBN 978-0-8130-8056-7 (pbk.)

The University Press of Florida is the scholarly publishing agency for the State University
System of Florida, comprising Florida A&M University, Florida Atlantic University, Florida
Gulf Coast University, Florida International University, Florida State University, New
College of Florida, University of Central Florida, University of Florida, University of North
Florida, University of South Florida, and University of West Florida.

University Press of Florida
2046 NE Waldo Road
Suite 2100
Gainesville, FL 32609
http://upress.ufl.edu

To Rachel and Charlie

There once was a crop
called Tobacco; once
there were sons, daughters, mothers,
fathers, neighbors;
there were popping and slapping sounds
and
stories swapped like work

SHELBY STEPHENSON,
"A HANDBOOK OF TOBACCO FARMING"

Contents

Figures

Acknowledgments

Like the farm families that occupy this book, I have learned that supportive kin and neighbors are a godsend. My family has been most helpful, so they deserve my first thanks. My wife, Rachel, has supported my work all along— even helping me go through stacks of materials in search of the tobacco farm families whose voices I sought—and made numerous sacrifices along the way. My son, Charlie, has put up with my writing and my distracted mind, too. I love them both for it. I also thank my dad and mom, George and Christine Bennett, whose stories about growing up in the rural South (although not on Tobacco Road) sent me searching.

Cindy Hahamovitch has been a source of sound advice and encouragement since before this project was even an idea. She is the mentor everyone should have. Thanks also to Kim Phillips, Judy Ewell, and Pete Daniel for guiding me as I started my now decade-long relationship with the history of the Tobacco South. Ray Arsenault and Gary Mormino really started me on the journey to being a historian. I am eternally grateful to them both.

This book originated as a seminar paper about my friend and colleague Buddy Paulett's family tobacco farm. I thank him for opening its history to me and inspiring this project. Thanks also to my other William & Mary friends: Dave Corlett, Kyle Zelner, Sarah Trembanis, Melissa Ooten, and Jennifer Oast.

Debra Reid and Jeannie Whayne both read drafts of this book and their comments made it better, as did an anonymous reader whose insightful suggestions about organization made this a much stronger (and more readable) book. I hope they like what I did with it. Rebecca Sharpless, Melissa Walker, Alex Lichtenstein, and Claire Strom all gave me opportunities to publish essays that let me think through some of ideas at the core of this book. I thank them all. Jeanette Keith, Lu Ann Jones, Douglas Hurt, John Inscoe, and Louis Kyriakoudes were all kind enough to comment on some of my attempts to present my ideas about tobacco farming in various venues. They, too, have made it better. I owe special thanks to Adrienne Petty and Monica Gisolfi for helping me get my work on some of those panels and for cheering this work along. Barbara Hahn, whose work on bright tobacco challenged and helped me in important ways, also deserves my thanks.

My colleagues in the history department at Florida Atlantic University have proved unfailing in their support, and I thank them all. Thanks especially to Talitha LeFlouria, Derrick White, and Kristen Block for listening to me think out loud. Thanks, too, to Patty Kollander, Steve Engle, and Mark Rose for mentoring me as both a scholar and teacher. Thanks, too, to Zella Linn, who keeps this whole place running.

I have been the happy recipient of a number of grants that helped support this work. The initial research was supported by the Lewis L. Glucksman Teaching Fellowship at the College of William & Mary and an Archie K. Davis Fellowship from the North Caroliniana Society. Later research was supported by a Betty Sams Christian Fellowship from the Virginia Historical Society. Thanks to all of these organizations for their support.

Finally, thanks to the helpful folks at the University Press of Florida for their aid in getting this book out. I owe special thanks to Meredith Morris-Babb and Sian Hunter for helping me get it into print and to Kate Babbitt for making it look right.

Introduction

A Hornworm's-Eye View of the Tobacco South

Carolina sphinx moths descend on tobacco fields at dusk in the late spring and early summer. They drink nectar from tobacco flowers and lay thousands of pearly eggs on the undersides of the maturing tobacco leaves. The caterpillars emerge three to five days later and are soon as green as the plants they feed on. They also develop a distinctive prong on their posteriors, making it obvious why they are better known as hornworms. Left alone, the insects can rapidly destroy the very leaves from which the farmer gains his profit. "The worms . . . would spend their days eating the leaves you were trying to sell," farmer William Hawthorne explained; controlling them was "a constant battle with nature . . . in a big plot in the hot sun."[1]

Difficult mostly because of the need to bend continuously in the sun for long hours, worming was both tedious and painstaking. "Endless labor" was one eighteenth-century observer's description; an "arduous task . . . that is never done," wrote a nineteenth-century planter. A farmer in the 1930s put it simply: "[It] ain't pleasant work."[2]

Perhaps because of its nastiness, worming is often in the forefront of the memories of those who have grown tobacco. Farmer Robert Hawthorne likely knew this when, in the presence of journalist Meg Medina, he bit a hornworm in two to the disgusted/delighted squeals of his daughter and nieces. He said he did it "purely for the crude entertainment of the help," but Medina surmised it went deeper than that. "He's counting on the power of family memories—even repulsive ones—to make at least one of these girls want to stay on this farm."[3]

The girls might have gained a hornworm story to tell their grandchildren, but the context for the story had changed entirely from those of earlier generations. Former slaves remembered worming with horror. Planters proved exacting in their demands that slaves, even children, give close attention to worming. Simon Stokes recalled that the overseer on the plantation where he grew up had "hawk eyes" for seeing worms on the tobacco and was quick to punish anyone who overlooked even a single worm. "You'd habe ter bite all de worms dat you miss, or git three lashes on yo' back wid his ole lash." Nancy Williams was five or six years old when she was sent to the fields to worm tobacco. Failing to heed a fellow slave's admonition to "pick 'em all off," she felt the wrath of her master when he noticed her carelessness. "[He] picked up a hand full of worms ... and stuffed 'em inter my mouth."[4]

These stories about hornworms reveal that the culture of agricultural work is time dependent, not inscribed in the crops themselves. Those who have grown tobacco might all remember hornworms, but they do not remember them in the same ways because the labor regimes they worked under mediated their experiences, and not just with worms. It really should be no surprise at all that workers separated by decades or centuries should remember things so differently.

But in the Tobacco South and in the rural South generally, memory often erodes difference and collapses experience. As activities such as worming become benign memories, they lose their context. Tobacco farming becomes a historical artifact, something quaint that should be revered and whose loss should be mourned. The loss of thousands of farms, the pressure of increasing global competition, and the scorn of a larger nonsmoking population have incubated a yearning in some to recast tobacco farms as centers of agrarian virtue and historical rootedness. "The people of tobacco, and those who live farm life exemplify the persevering spirit of America," one artist has written. Both Virginia and North Carolina have given semi-official endorsement to this sentiment by offering motorists specialty license plates touting each state's "Tobacco Heritage." Even hornworms have their place in sustaining this memory: hornworm races held during the annual Harvest Festival at North Carolina's Duke Homestead State Historic Site invite children to experience the gross joys of handling the caterpillars.[5]

In the rush to use tobacco as a portal to an imagined past, artists and writers obscure a much more complex history. *When Tobacco Was King* offers a corrective to such reductive views of tobacco agriculture in the U.S. South. Closely examining the spaces where work, nature, and culture come together, it maps the transformation of tobacco work from the end of slavery to the present day. Its overarching argument is that there is little about the post–Civil War rural South that was stable, even the region's seemingly venerable family farms. Hardly timeless, family labor was a product of late-nineteenth-century compromises about how staple crops could be grown in the wake of emancipation, and from the beginning this method of arranging work was shaky at best. Low prices and outmigration placed constant pressures on tobacco farming families. Indeed, it was only the creation of the Federal Tobacco Program in the 1930s that gave family farms any semblance of stability. But the program's protections could go only so far in the face of new pressures unleashed in the post–World War II era, when mechanization, globalization, and neoliberal economic policies destabilized the family agricultural model. Like the decades following emancipation, the last three decades or so have been a time of reordering, a time when family farms have largely been replaced by large-scale operations dependent on hired labor, much of it from other shores.

When Tobacco Was King examines this transformation in a particular part of the South. The Old Bright Belt is a diverse region in the Virginia–North Carolina Piedmont that forms a rough rectangle with Danville, Virginia, at its center. The region gets its name from the bright, or flue-cured, variety of tobacco it spawned. Piedmont planters developed the techniques for making the variety, which is noted for the curiously yellow color of the cured leaves, in the mid-nineteenth century. Following the Civil War, manufacturers offered high prices for the rare bright leaves and farm families across the Piedmont adopted the crop and its regimens to meet this demand. While farmers in eastern North Carolina (the New Bright Belt) and South Carolina had begun to grow the variety by the turn of the twentieth century (followed by farmers in Georgia and Florida by the time of World War I), bright tobacco agriculture was first defined in the Piedmont.[6]

The work that follows examines the history of tobacco agriculture in the Old Bright Belt across the long twentieth century, from emancipation to the abandonment of federal crop controls in 2004. It focuses especially on the work of growing tobacco because work offers the best context for understanding the profound forces that have remade the U.S. South over the last century. While the impact of modernization is inscribed in the landscapes and demographics of the modern South, understanding the cultural and political ramifications of that process requires that we examine the everyday lives of rural southerners for whom work was central. Viewed this way,

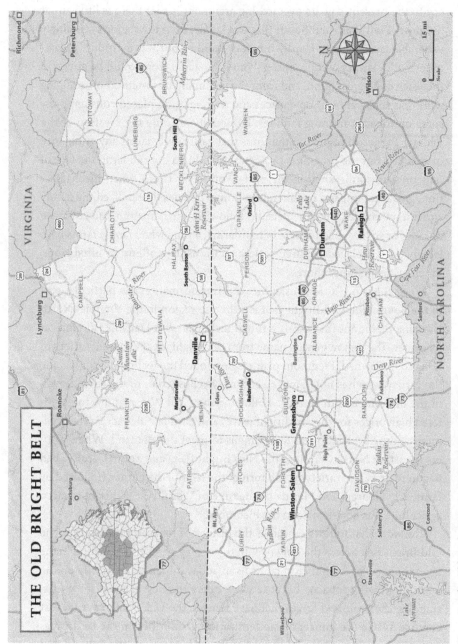

Figure I.1. The Old Bright Belt. Cartography by Mapcraft.com.

the wrenching of millions from the countryside is far more dramatic than statistics can tell. It is obvious that it was far from the inevitable product of mechanization or globalization. Instead, we see that government and corporate leaders and farm families shaped modernization in ways that reflected their own interests and defined its contours. Instead of an inexorable phenomenon, modernization was the result of competing ideologies—capitalism, producerism, democracy, corporatism—applied to the countryside.

Examining labor reminds us that agricultural modernization did not really lead to a final destination. For all the depictions of the modern South as a land of superhighways, suburbs, and strip malls, agriculture remains a critical shaper of the region's political economy. Southerners may grow less tobacco and cotton than they once did and fewer southerners may work in agriculture, but agricultural producers still wield considerable political and economic power across the region. Sugar growers, poultry aggregators, vegetable farmers, soybean farmers, and tobacco growers continue to shape politics, public policy, and labor relations in their respective parts of the South.[7]

When Tobacco Was King begins with the greatest labor disruption in U.S. history: emancipation. For nearly two centuries, tobacco culture in North America was defined by slavery and inequality. Planters extracted wealth from the reproductive power of the soil and bodies they owned and defined themselves by their ability to manage both. After emancipation, they found it difficult to harness either. Freedpeople refused to work in gangs and demanded land and whatever dignities and protections it might give them. At the same time, small white farmers discovered that evolutions in the tobacco market—the growing popularity of bright tobacco and the expansion of the loose-leaf tobacco auction—democratized their access to markets that had long excluded them. Drawn in by the promise of a good living from a few acres, they joined former slaves in growing bright tobacco. Together, albeit not exactly in concert, their farms eclipsed the plantation as the predominant site of tobacco production.

These small landowners and tenants worked with their own hands and turned to their wives, children, extended kin, and even neighbors for the additional labor they needed. As they worked together, they created a new tobacco culture, one that esteemed knowledge gained from working hard. Egalitarian in its ethos if not in its performance (patriarchy shaped its assumptions of power, as did racism and class), it created spaces for those outside the plantation ideal to prove their worth.

They could also demonstrate it on the auction warehouse floors, where neighbors and strangers witnessed the sale of tobacco. A strange and exciting world, the auctions nevertheless revealed their weakness vis-à-vis manufacturers, especially after 1890, when the American Tobacco Company dominated the market and drove prices down. The hope for high prices never faded, but they became all the more rare.

Insulting prices, as families saw them, rubbed up against their developing sense of worth, sparking repeated protests. From the 1870s to the 1920s, they sought to shape national agrarian organizations such as the Grange, the Farmers' Alliance, and the Farmers' Union to counter the markets. When those failed, they made their own organizations and grounded them in the egalitarianism born of their experiences. These, too, proved too weak to make any changes.

In the 1920s, the disappointment of falling back on hard times after a brief period of high prices brought on by wartime demand pushed them to organize again, this time in the hope of monopolizing the market for themselves. Entire families joined the Tri-State Tobacco Growers' Cooperative. Although that organization proved too unwieldy and weak to solve their problems, the federal government proved strong enough to limit production and set prices. The New Deal's Federal Tobacco Program controlled production and raised prices while defending small-scale production. If it was not exactly what farm families had wanted, it was close enough, and they clung to it for seventy years because of the protections it offered.

By mid-century, however, its weaknesses had become apparent. Production controls reduced the ability of families to support themselves on a few acres. Thousands gave up, drawn by the promise of higher wages or cleaner work in cities and their growing suburbs. For those that remained, the need for labor pressed ever harder. New machines helped, but they also hindered, obviating the need for workers in some seasons, but not in others. These workers, especially farm women, whose time was suddenly better spent in factories or teaching or just about anywhere else, were now absent in the seasons when equipment was of limited help.

To replace them, families increasingly turned to hired workers, including migrants and imported immigrants with little connection to the Old Bright Belt or tobacco. As these new tobacco workers learned how to top and sucker and prime and cure, they reshaped the relationships between landowners and workers. The mutuality that had held families and neighbors together faded, replaced by impersonal connections between labor and management.

Farm families might celebrate the heritage of family in the leaves, but the real work of growing tobacco depended on the hands of strangers.

The globalization of the Old Bright Belt's workforce coincided with the globalization of the cigarette market in the latter half of the twentieth century, a change that swamped the Federal Tobacco Program. By the 1980s, large growers had begun to question the need for the program and its controls. They chafed at its limits and the costs of keeping domestic prices inflated. They hoped, instead, to jettison it for the free market, so they might better compete with non-U.S. growers on the global market. Growing alliances with the tobacco companies, driven in large part by the politics of cigarettes and cancer, convinced them further that the program had outlived its usefulness.

Even then, though, leading growers and their political allies continued to feel the tug of the mutuality and support for small farm families that had shaped the program from its inception. They wanted the program gone, but they did not want it to mean that retired farmers would be impoverished by the loss of their ability to lease the quotas the Federal Tobacco Program had given them. So they engineered a $10 billion buyout to guarantee they would see something for their rights. At the dawn of another century, the buyout has reshaped the Old Bright Belt again. What it will look like remains to be seen. The only sure thing is that tobacco will reign no more.

1

Family

Rural economists came to Charlotte County, Virginia, in 1922 to learn about raising tobacco. In particular, they wanted to measure the work farmers did in the hope that they might resolve the persistent poverty of the South's bright tobacco belts. They confirmed mathematically what farmers already knew in their legs and backs and hands: growing tobacco was hard work. Charlotte County bright tobacco farms were small—the average farm in the study had only six acres in the crop—but the process of getting it from seed to sale took a year or more and required upward of 430 person-hours of labor per acre. Half the expense in growing an acre of tobacco would be in labor costs alone, the researchers figured, if the average farmer had to hire workers. But most farmers did not. "The labor used in producing a crop is furnished almost entirely by the operator and his family," the researchers explained.[1]

Others noted a similar pattern throughout the region. Children were "helping their fathers with the crops," one observer wrote in 1926, because "hired labor is practically non-existent here." Another noted that because of a "shortage of labor . . . the boys and girls had to take the place of laborers and 'see the crop thro.'" Other researchers inverted the causal relationship and stripped family labor of its romanticism. It was not simply that hired laborers were scarce, they suggested, but that with "family help" available, "many farmers used the labor of members of their families without paying any direct wage." Helping, in other words, was just working for free.[2]

Farm families likely would not have depicted their work in such starkly economic terms. Most saw their work as an extension of the household economy, not as part of the larger public economy. Wives and children were the primary labor force for an entire economy. Following emancipation, the bulk of tobacco production in the Piedmont shifted from the plantation, where gangs of slaves worked under strict planter oversight, to individual house-holds, where husbands and fathers, landowners and sharecroppers exploited both their own labor and that of the their families to produce bright tobacco.

Most accounts of southern agriculture in the twentieth century either take the widespread use of unpaid family labor for granted or fall back on a ver-sion of the explanation offered by contemporary observers: growing tobacco required everyone in the family to help. But crops really only require a few things, none of which is a specific way of organizing labor. The limits of crop production are largely natural ones—water, soil, climate—but the arrange-ment of labor is a product of how people decide to meet not only the biologi-cal requirements of the plants but also the anthropocentric requirements of the market. Tobacco no more forced wives and children into the fields than it had forced slaves and indentured servants into the fields before them. The cen-trality of family labor to tobacco production in the Piedmont was neither nat-ural nor preordained; it was a product of historical development. Any number of ways of organizing labor could have developed in the years following the Civil War, but the confluence of the breakdown of the plantation system, the increased demand for bright tobacco, the availability of cheap land that could support bright tobacco agriculture, and the expansion of the tobacco market by eager capitalists set the stage for the dominance of family labor.

Emancipation initiated the transition to family farming. Without slaves, the plantation model faltered. After visiting Richmond in 1870, journalist Robert Somers declared that Virginia's agricultural future was the "absorbing ques-tion" for most in the state. "How to get the estates formerly productive again brought into cultivation . . . occupies the minds of all classes with an intensity of interest to which no other public concern can be compared." In the South-side, where tobacco had driven the economy before the war, commercial ag-riculture continued to lag in the years after the war. By 1870, the number of improved acres was far below that of 1860. Hardest hit were the plantation counties, where tobacco production was 40 percent of that of 1860.[3]

At the same time, the center of U.S. tobacco agriculture appeared to be shifting westward, from Virginia and North Carolina to Kentucky and Ten-nessee, where growers were able to take advantage of better connections to northern manufacturers. In the 1870s alone, Kentucky farmers nearly dou-bled their tobacco production, driving prices down for the crops Virginia and North Carolina planters could get to market.[4]

Ecological problems also bedeviled Virginia and North Carolina tobacco planters. Landowners returning from the Civil War had to contend with silted creeks and gullied hills made worse by years of deforestation and shallow tillage, two hallmarks of antebellum tobacco agriculture. A writer identified only as "H" put it bluntly: "Southside Virginia and North Carolina, throughout the Tobacco region, present a scarred and naked surface." Abandoned fields reclaimed by nature also challenged farmers. As late as 1875, an "Old Fogy" at Hampden-Sydney College in Prince Edward County, Virginia, complained that "creek and branch bottoms are converted into swamps and marshes; hills and slopes . . . are covered with briers and sassafrass [sic] and pines. . . . Clover . . . has almost disappeared, and broomsedge and hen-grass at once disfigure the face and proclaim the barrenness of fields which, before the war, bore heavy growths of cultivated grasses or natural vegetation." Successive droughts burned tobacco plants in the field, while nematodes and fungal infections brought on by repeated use of the same fields—a product of the dearth of labor to clear new ones—ruined the roots.[5]

In the minds of agricultural elites, putting freedpeople back to work in the fields was the key to resolving the agricultural crisis. The idea that tobacco could be grown only by black workers remained an article of faith for some planters. "All those people who say they would not take back their slaves if they could are kin to Baron Munchhausen," Mecklenburg County, North Carolina, planter C. D. Whittle wrote in 1867. "I am no kith [to Munchhausen] & [I] want mine." Two decades later, another planter spoke of the supposed necessity of black workers. "I must have niggers to work for me," he exclaimed. "I can't do nothing on my place without 'em. If they send all the niggers to Africa, I'll have to go thar, too." Elites largely rejected the idea of simply turning land over to African American tenants, however. Stories about the "improvidence of the negro" appeared regularly in agricultural publications, warning farmers not to allow black farmers to work without direct oversight.[6]

When they did rent land to freedpeople, planters sought as much control over black workers as possible. Share contracts often obligated black workers far beyond the tasks related directly to the crop to be divided. In December 1865, William J. Berryman and James M. Williams, partners who were renting a farm in Pittsylvania County, Virginia, secured a contract with two freedmen identified only as Gary and Amos. In return for half of the crops and the use of a team of mules (for farm work only, the contract insisted), Gary and Amos agreed to provide all of the labor and half of the costs of supplies necessary for making crops of tobacco, oats, and corn. The contract also called for them to haul wood for Berryman and Williams and till their garden plot. Meanwhile, Gary and Amos's own garden plot was to be "simply a garden for the cultivation of vegetables to be used upon the premises," not for vegetables they could sell.[7]

Planters often also expected male sharecroppers to make their female kin work in other women's houses. In return for the rent-free house they would occupy, Gary and Amos were also "to furnish two women" to cook, wash clothes, clean, make beds, draw water, milk cows, and churn butter for Berryman and Williams and their families. One Granville County, North Carolina, planter urged his peers to make agreements that required "the laborer . . . to furnish the employer with the service of a woman so many days in the year" so they could secure not just domestic labor also but "extra labor when the condition of their crops required it." William T. Sutherlin of Pittsylvania County envisioned turning freedpeople into something like serfs. Establish "negro laborers on a place," he told an audience in 1867, "creating in their minds feelings of local attachment and domiciliary influences." "These laborers would form a sort of peasantry" that would give landowners "the best assurance of obtaining labor."[8]

Dominance remained a chief goal for white elites. In Virginia, Charlotte County planter George Hannah offered his former slaves annual contracts that required that they "work diligently & faithfully, obeying all orders . . . promptly every day during the said year, complying fully with all the rules & regulations . . . for the government of their work and deportment." Halifax County, Virginia, planter Robert L. Ragland advised others to maintain the control and air of mastery that had been hallmarks of plantation management. "They should be treated kindly, but *firmly*," he wrote to potential employers. "Have but few words with them, and these on business. Use no familiarity, and instinct will cause them to look up to you." He also demanded that workers labor in gangs, as had been common during slavery, and be directed by a system of bells or horns. "On no people on earth does this system operate better or more availingly than upon the negro," he opined. Ed Currin, remembered using such techniques to manage both the farm hands and sharecroppers on the Granville County, North Carolina, farm he purchased in the 1880s. "They all knowed I was square, and I expected them to be. I wouldn't stand no cussin', and I was the boss of my land. What they didn't know how to do, I showed 'em. I had a big bell hangin' in the back yard to ring for them, and the whole neighborhood set its clocks by it." Person County, North Carolina, farmer A. J. Hester's attempt at installing a similar system of bells was less successful. The "Negroes were prejudiced to this system," a reporter noted; "[it] looked too much like slavery."[9]

In the face of such resistance, some landlords insisted on using violence, as planters had done before emancipation. In 1865, Freedmen's Bureau agents in Lynchburg found it necessary to issue orders "to prevent persons employing freedmen from assaulting them with sticks and stones, for what they term insolence." In 1867, freedman William Price of Caswell County, North Carolina, reported that he had been "brutally treated" by the supervisor on the plantation where he was working. That same year, an audience asked William T. Sutherlin what he would do if "a negro . . . refused to comply with his contract, neglected his business, and became rebellious." Sutherlin replied that "he never had but one such instance, and then, his overseer knocked the fellow down" to assert that such a "remedy" was "part of the contract." B. F. Hester of Granville County claimed he never had to resort to violence, but he nevertheless approached his relations with the workers on 1,200-acre farm with the same firmness. "When they fail to comply with their contract, [he] settles with them and they are told to 'git up and git,'" recounted a reporter.[10]

Black workers resisted whites' attempts to exert such close control over their labor and that of their families. Some sought to escape the oversight of employers by avoiding working for whites entirely. In January 1866, the Freedmen's Bureau assistant superintendent for Amelia County, Virginia, reported that he had received "frequent complaints" about freedpeople squatting on or renting poor or abandoned land in the hope of subsisting on small patches of corn and vegetables, despite the fact that "farmers were begging for laborers, offering 7, 8 & 10 dollars p[e]r month or one fourth the crop with everything furnished." Interested to learn more, he personally made the rounds, finding in "an old tobacco barn three families on a dirt floor, Six grown persons and ten children, with as they said provisions to last about half the year . . . , intending to clear up the land and make a crop with the hoe on the poorest of land and pay one fourth rent." "I know that the three men living in the tobacco barn were offered a place on one of the best farms in the county," he added, astonished that the freedpeople "refused, preferring to dig a crop out and pay rent." His attempt to force these people off the land and into labor contracts ultimately failed.[11]

Other freedpeople resisted with their feet and took jobs building railroads or moved out of the region entirely on the promise of higher wages in the Deep South. The *Lynchburg Republican* noted in January 1870 that "a freight train on the Southside Road brought up yesterday 164 negroes from the southside counties, mainly from Halifax, and the adjacent Counties of Persons [sic] and Granville, North Carolina" on their way to Alabama and Louisiana.[12]

Those who agreed to work for white landowners resisted their attempts to pay poverty wages. In 1866, newspapers as far away as Georgia carried reports that black workers in Caswell County had "held meetings in two different places" and "passed resolutions to the effect that they would not work during the ensuing year for less than $150 and board, the quantity and quality of the provisions to be prescribed by themselves." The assistant commissioner of the Freedmen's Bureau in North Carolina reported that freedpeople throughout the state generally demanded monthly contracts from planters, who offered annual ones in order to exert greater control over the mobility of black workers but sometimes refused to honor them. "The laborer says 'you fool me long enough'; 'you promise but you never pay.'"[13]

Black people's assertion of their right to control their labor coincided, and sometimes fueled, political upheaval in the Virginia and North Carolina Piedmont. In the late 1860s, the Ku Klux Klan instigated a wave of terror in North Carolina's Piedmont counties. The Klan assaulted African Americans primarily for their support of the Republican Party, but the violence was also sparked by changing labor relations. Rumors that freedpeople had conspired to burn landlords' barns played on whites' fears of the loss of control over black workers. The Klan scourged and shot a number of African Americans in Alamance and Orange counties for supposedly burning barns, and in 1870, members killed white Republican leader John Stephens in Caswell County after accusing him of telling black Union League members to burn white farmers' tobacco barns. The Klan also attacked labor recruiters in Caswell County.[14]

The violence made white fears of black mobility something of a self-fulfilling prophecy. African Americans moved from the countryside into well-established cities such as Richmond, Virginia, and Raleigh, North Carolina and the growing cities of the Piedmont in hopes of finding better work and escaping the violence. According to Caswell Holt, a freedman who was twice attacked by masked white men, "a great many" blacks in Alamance and surrounding counties "will not live out in the country at all, because they are afraid to stay anywhere out of town." Person County's black population fell by more than 7 percent between 1860 and 1870, and Alamance County's black population dropped by nearly 6 percent; in Virginia, Brunswick County had nearly 10 percent fewer blacks by 1870, while Lunenburg County's black population fell by an astonishing 20 percent during the decade.[15]

Protests forced white landowners to accommodate black demands. In the 1870s, increasing numbers of landowners decided to rent their land to African Americans, who, in turn, perhaps saw tenancy as something of a compromise in an era of political and economic hard times. By 1880, when tenancy was first measured, the practice was most widespread in the former plantation counties with the largest black populations. The availability of land, however constrained, reversed the postwar exodus; in the fifteen years since emancipation, the black population in the Virginia–North Carolina Piedmont grew by nearly 40 percent. A considerable part of the increase was due to growing populations in urban areas, but rural counties grew as well. In fact, many of the rural counties that witnessed an exodus during the 1860s experienced double-digit growth rates in the 1870s.

It was not the outflow of workers alone that changed landowners' minds about black tenants; changes in crop lien laws also strengthened their control over tenants. In 1873, Virginia legislators passed the state's first lien law, giving landowners first claim over crops produced on their land. Two years later, North Carolina's politicians rewrote its lien law to give landowners not only the first claim but also absolute possession of crops produced by tenants. The laws effectively treated shares as deferred wages under the control of the landowner until the completion of the contract at the end of the year. Landlords could, and did, abuse the system with impunity, and many share contracts stipulated that croppers work additional hours for the landowner or do other tasks unrelated to the cash crops. But most black families found these terms to be preferable to working for wages, at least full time, because it allowed them some relative autonomy. For black men, the ability to exercise greater control over the labor of their wives and children was especially attractive because it could save them from the abuse many suffered while working directly for white men.[16]

Landowners' changing views of the land also opened the door for change. Some simply did not wish to worry about the management of laborers, and managing sharecropping and rental contracts was far easier than managing farm hands, especially for some women landowners. Others simply had no desire to stay in rural areas, and in a migration not unlike that of their former slaves, moved to urban areas. "We call upon our native white people to be content with their country and remain here," one newspaper editor pleaded in 1883. "Don't let your freehold in this fair land slip from you, to be grasped and held by foreign and colored settlers." To Sallie Bruce's consternation, many did not listen. "All the ladies and gentlemen are disappearing from this country and in twenty years there will be none left in this section I am sure," she lamented from Charlotte County. Another writer pondered whether turning from tobacco to grapes might forestall the elite exodus by "keeping at home our young men, and especially our young *gentlemen*, who are now going south and to the cities." Armistead Burwell, who had once complained bitterly of a distant relative who had decided to abandon "his duty to take care of his father's family" and move to bustling Oxford, North Carolina, fretted that his own kin might give up his family's ancestral Mecklenburg County land. "If I should never marry," he wrote to his brother, "I expect to leave [your son] the old homestead, on condition of [him] living at it, and never selling it."[17]

A growing pool of white farm families eager to rent land may have convinced landowners to adopt tenancy. White tenancy was nothing new in the Piedmont; landless white families operated almost one-quarter of the farms in central North Carolina before the Civil War. Leading planters encouraged fellow landowners to expand the practice of renting to white farmers if they were planning to give up everyday management of their lands. The Census Bureau did not enumerate white tenants separately from black tenants until 1900, but results from that year showed that whites operated roughly three-fifths of the region's sharecropped farms. Even in a place like Halifax County, Virginia, where more than half of the population was black, the majority of tenants were white.[18]

The growing popularity of bright tobacco in the 1870s and after also convinced landowners to turn to tenants and sharecroppers. Bright tobacco promised high prices, but the techniques used to produce it required even closer attention and more labor than the dark-fired tobacco of earlier generations. Unlike eighteenth-century planters, who bought slaves and built plantations in response to high tobacco prices, landowners decentralized production and put the risk on the backs of tenant families, who would have to manage their own labor if they hoped to make any profit at the end of the year.

In general, landowners rented land in two ways: they offered three-quarters of the crop to tenants who provided their own stock and implements, and they offered half the crop to those who had no stock or implements (croppers) in exchange for their labor. Actual contracts could be far more complex. In the 1930s, sociologist Margaret Jarman Hagood noted that "the range of tenure classifications extends from a few who pay standing rent, cash or produce, to the sharecroppers who get two-thirds of everything he raises, with all sorts of intermediate rental practices." She added, "There are some inversions of the usual negative relationship between rental fractions and economic level, however. The most prosperous-appearing family visited pays one-half to their landlord, while a destitute family pays nothing to an owner who supplies them a house and land for patches since the old man . . . is too feeble to 'tend land' any longer."[19]

Observers noted that many landlords were absentees, and "a good more supervision is given in the coastal plain area than in the Piedmont." (Share-cropping was more prevalent on the coastal plain.) Samuel C. Hubbard stip-ulated that his tenant P. H. Layne plant 125,000 hills of tobacco, cultivate all of the corn, oat, and wheat land, and pay for three-fourths of the fertilizer bill, as well as store up manure, clean the farm's ditches, and trim the hedges that ran along the farm's riverbank. When Layne failed to follow the contract, Hubbard sued him. Hubbard, however, only learned of Layne's shortcomings when Layne admitted to another man that he had planted less than half of the tobacco stipulated in the contract. "It would be well for you to prove by some one or two good men in the neighborhood who saw Layne's crop on your land while it was growing as to the probable value of it," Hubbard's at-torney advised him.[20]

Like Layne, tenants often controlled the pace of work on their farms, oversaw all of the tasks, and even sold their crops at market. There were lim-its, though. Black tenants often faced greater restrictions than white tenants, and landlords watched sharecroppers closer than renters. Landowners, one Virginian explained, preferred croppers "for reason the landlord has more control."[21]

Black farmer Arthur Barnes's experiences with numerous landlords in Granville and Durham Counties during the early twentieth century reveal much about the vagaries and complexities of tenants' lives. At seventeen, Barnes had to leave the farm he had grown up on when his father died and the owner sold the property. "I wanted more land. I seen where I had a big family and could use more land, and the new owner wouldn't give it to me because I was a boy." He sharecropped on Robert Thompson's 800-acre "plantation." "I had plenty of land but didn't have the horsepower to work it. I used his stock and he fed it; I paid half the fertilizer and we split what the crop brought." The following year he moved on to Charley Powell's land. "He gimme a good chance; I cleared 600 dollars on a 2,000 dollar crop," Barnes recalled. "My next oldest brother worked for wages, and all the rest helped me." The following year he "rented a whole plantation for standing rent, 100 dollars a year, and paid part of that in advance." A bad crop left him "600 dollars in the hole," forcing him to sell his horses. He moved on to Mark Lang's property, where he stayed only one year because of the death of his wife and infant child. Barnes moved in with his mother and siblings to work on Harvey Martin's land. "He had about 1,500 acres . . . and wouldn't rent noway but on shares. . . . Mr. Martin would furnish stock or else feed yours. He was a fertilizer dealer, too, and he was awful free to furnish his people all through the year, but when fall came he got the big end of the horn; in the windup most of the people on his place owed him all they made." Unsatisfied, he moved the next year to a Mr. Jackson's land, where he finished out a crop started by another tenant. "I used Mr. Jackson's mules and made a splendid crop." While Barnes cast his movements as a rational choice, it was clear that he and other tenants were at the mercy of landowners. "One reason you move around so much is you get land in cultivation and then the man will want the land, and rather than cultivate new land or old land grown up with little pines and broomsedge you move on to another place."[22]

As Barnes's depiction of field rotation suggests, the land itself reinforced complex landlord-tenant relations. The region's rolling topography and highly variable soil types made the land something of a patchwork of desirable farmland. Tenants were often at some distance from landlords, and landowners themselves often rented land, sometimes on the same terms as sharecroppers, to cobble enough land together for their fickle tobacco crops. This created intricate webs of land tenure that are masked by tenancy rates calculated from census returns. Individuals the census counted as tenant farmers often owned pieces of land that were either too small or had less desirable soil. Some landowners rented their land to others even as they rented other lands. "I have been renting land pay ¼ for rent," explained Sampson White, a black farmer from Pittsylvania County in 1910. "I also work a farm of my own and had been for 9 years. I work men for a part of the crop and they pay ½ the fertilizer bill and gets ½ of the crop. I work land of my own and rent land and rent out land to others."[23]

Work patterns were similarly complex and revealed the limits landowners could place on their tenants. In the busiest seasons, landowners paid cash to experienced farm hands, white and black, so tenants found opportunities to work on other people's farms. Those adept at curing tobacco could charge neighbors for their services. Many farm women, black and white, strung tobacco bags for manufacturers at home to supplement their families' incomes. Mrs. Emma Mitchell, a black farm woman from Rockingham County, earned almost $25 per week stringing bags in 1939; enough, one researcher noted, to "make her living by this work alone." Her earnings helped her farming family buy a car, a piano, a radio, and a sewing machine and build a new ten-room house.[24]

Others took off-farm work, or "public work," in the region's growing textile and tobacco factories. For white families, splitting time between the farm and public work was common. Since the need for labor in some factories was tied to agricultural production, many families timed their public work to fit the seasonal demands of the farm. Husbands or older sons might spend part of the year in factories, on railroads, or in tobacco warehouses, while wives and daughters might spend another part of the year in factories. One North Carolina woman recalled that her parents shared work at the Dan River Cotton Mill in Danville, Virginia, in order to make ends meet. In the winter, her father commuted from the farm to work on the looms, while in the summer, her mother took his place so he could work in the fields.[25]

Black workers had fewer opportunities to take factory work, but the few jobs available became lifelines for numerous farm families. One historian has noted that in Winston, many of the town's "black factory workers remained firmly rooted to their homes in other areas." According to another historian, Durham's tobacco factories needed stemmers only in the months immediately following the harvest, which allowed the black women who worked in the stemmeries to split their time between farm and factory. Black men often worked in the warehouses where they and others sold their tobacco.[26]

The power of landowners was further weakened by the availability of credit for tenant farmers. Banks in Durham, Winston-Salem, Greensboro, Raleigh, and Danville provided access to credit outside the crop lien. A 1934 study found that these banks, rather than merchants, were important sources of capital for many farmers. "Crop liens are not used as much," the author noted. Black farmers had their own, albeit much smaller, banks. At various times before 1920, there were black-owned banks in Durham, Winston-Salem, Petersburg, Danville, and Richmond. Tobacco warehouses, too, would sometimes extend credit to black farmers who promised to bring them business. "The average negro farmer has no trouble getting loans," a white Extension Service agent complained in 1919, "so he will not work for the white man."[27]

The availability of credit supported the growth in landownership in the

Piedmont's former plantation counties. By the turn of the twentieth century, the majority of farm operators in these counties owned the farms they worked on. Most farms were small. In Granville and neighboring North Carolina counties, the number of farms increased grew by more than 350 percent between 1860 and 1920 even as improved acreage fell by a fifth over the same period: between 1880 (the first year the census differentiated between owner- and tenant-operated farms) and 1920, the number of owner-operated farms increased by 69 percent. Just across the state line in Mecklenburg County, the number of farms increased by more than 500 percent between 1860 and 1920, while the number of owner-operated farms more than doubled between 1880 and 1920.[28]

The breakdown of the plantation system led many landowners to sell at least some of their property. As early as 1867, observers noted "a prevalent disposition" in many parts of Virginia "to sell all surplus area of farms above 100 to 200 acres." In other cases, speculators moved in and subdivided former plantations and then, with the support of tobacco warehousemen, promoted the land to potential settlers. According to one promoter, the best lands in Granville County went for $40 per acre, but less desirable land could be had for $5 to $7 per acre in 1887. At an 1895 auction, "farmers in the neighborhood," hoping to expand their holdings, bought subdivided lands for $10 to $20 per acre. Observers noted similar prices in neighboring counties. Armistead Burwell was especially angered by speculators who took advantage of a glutted market in land. "Mr. Overby . . . was busy all the time cutting up and selling land to negroes at $10 per acre which cost $2," Burwell wrote to his brother in 1891. "It will of course ruin the neighborhood but he cares not for that so long as there is money in it for him."[29]

At the time of his death in 1920, Armistead Burwell may have been surprised (or not) to know that there were more black landowners in his census tract than white ones. According to historian Loren Schweninger, "former slaves and their children [in Virginia] became almost obsessed with the idea of acquiring their own land."[30] The same could be said of their North Carolina neighbors. Former slave Mattie Curtis bought fifteen acres of overgrown fields in Granville County from a land company and then cleared the land herself. "I cut down the big trees that was all over these fields and I mauled out the wood and sold it, then I plowed up the fields and planted them."[31] By 1920, many former plantation counties, especially in Virginia, had rates of black farm ownership near or above 50 percent. Many were small tracts where black farm families practiced subsistence agriculture as a means of supplementing wages from laboring or sharecropping on white-owned farms. These small farms offered a degree of independence that was unavailable to the landless.[32]

Whites sometimes resented this independence and intimidated blacks who owned land. In Vance County, North Carolina, local whites killed a black farm family and burned their house to the ground for what the NAACP's magazine *The Crisis* described as "the new crime of landowning." There were enough exceptions to belie any rule about black landowners, however, and many were able to build farms that lasted generations.[33]

Just as the expansion of tenancy and small landownership reshaped the connection between land and labor in the region's former plantation counties, thousands of farm families reshaped neighboring counties, traditionally counties where plantations had been fewer, especially in North Carolina. Land speculators sold thousands of acres of once sparsely populated but not necessarily marginal land to farmers, promising them a fresh start.

At the same time, thousands of landowners, even relatively small ones, oriented their farms toward the tobacco market and hired sharecroppers and tenants to work on land they could not give attention to. In the Blue Ridge foothills, both the number of farms and the number of improved acres increased rapidly after 1880. Patrick County, Virginia, had nearly 70 percent more improved acreage in 1920 than it had in 1880 and almost four times as many farms. Across the state line in Stokes County, North Carolina, improved acreage increased by more than two-thirds and the number of farms doubled, while in neighboring Surry County, North Carolina, the number of improved acres nearly doubled and the number of farms increased by nearly threefold. Others found opportunities in the counties south of the region's traditional tobacco counties. In North Carolina, in the line of counties running from Durham in the east to Forsyth in the west, the number of farms grew by more than 55 percent and improved acreage increased by 15 percent between 1880 and 1920.

In these areas, especially in the western counties, whites made up the vast majority of both landowners and sharecroppers, but black farm families found some room as well. "[A] great many colored people have right smart little farms in Virginia," a black railroad worker from Campbell County, Virginia, told congressional investigators in 1883. "I know a man named Jackson that has had three farms, and he has two now," he continued. "I don't know what they cost him, but . . . one of them is 300 acres."[34] Although Surry County's black population was still small, it doubled between 1860 and 1900.

Cheap land no doubt drew many. By 1920, nearly two-thirds of black farmers in the county owned the land they worked. By that same year, two-fifths of black farmers in Orange County, North Carolina, owned their farms, while more than half in Forsyth County did. In Chatham County, Temple Herndon Durham and her husband Exter made the jump from sharecroppers to landowners sometime in the late nineteenth century. "We paid a hundred dollars we done saved," she told an interviewer in the 1930s.[35]

Widespread landownership increased the pace of the reorientation of tobacco farm labor to family units. Lacking capital, both tenants and small landowners relied on their families to do the work instead of hiring workers with any regularity. A survey by the North Carolina Department of Labor found that by 1916, farmers in only five of the state's eighteen Old Bright Belt counties hired workers. In 1919, more than 80 percent of Old Bright Belt farmers reported that they hired no labor at all, and of those that did, each paid out an average of only $166 in wages for the year, including wages paid in housing rather than in cash. By the second decade of the twentieth century, wage labor was largely a seasonal phenomenon, undertaken largely by local people looking to add to the income their own crops could bring. Family workers overwhelmingly pulled the load for most of the year. More than the physical division of land, this new labor regime marked the birth of the Old Bright Belt.[36]

2

Hands

Asked about growing tobacco in the 1930s, black farmer Walter Corbett put it simply: "A man can't raise tobacco without children to help." Much could separate the material conditions of life for croppers, tenants, and small landowners, but work was not one of them. On most Old Bright Belt farms, entire families did the work of growing tobacco. From spring to fall, they labored together in the fields and around the barns. Fathers and husbands most often exerted strong control over the labor of wives and children, but many found joy in the work. "When I was a girl, I helped plant tobacco, sucker it, pick off the worms, and everything else," one Virginia woman recalled of growing up in the early twentieth century. "My papa said he lost his best hand when I got married," a white tenant woman told sociologist Margaret Jarman Hagood in the 1930s. Farm families might hire help in the busiest seasons, but most saw their crops through by sharing labor with neighbors and extended kin.[1]

Agricultural elites looked askance at such labor arrangements. In the late nineteenth century, large farmers and former planters decried the sight of white women and children in the fields and argued that black workers were best suited for tobacco work. (They, of course, felt no compunction about employing black women and children.) By the early twentieth century, government experts saw in family labor the very inefficiencies they described as the bane of good agriculture. An extension agent's description of women and children "slaving in the tobacco fields" captured their impression of family labor well.[2]

Farm women and children likely would have taken exception to such depictions of their work. They would have depicted their work in much more positive terms, as would their husbands and fathers. For most, tobacco had insinuated itself into their identity. Some who grew up in tobacco have written eloquently, if perhaps romantically, of the identity forged in the fields. "To me, this was a good kind of life," Kentuckian Wendell Berry has written. "To work in the company of men and women who were superb workers, to learn their characters, to glean from their talk an intimate history of the people, farms, and fields that were one's true nationality—this was an indispensable education." North Carolinian Billy Yeargin put it more succinctly. "What do the tobacco fields represent to me now? Not just an age-old way of life, but life itself."[3]

The mythos of the family farm is an old one with roots deep in the nation's history. It and its meaning are not timeless, however. Farmers have rearticulated it again and again, in response to particular historical circumstances. In the Old Bright Belt, the transition to a family-centered model of tobacco labor opened an opportunity for a new articulation. As families and neighbors worked daily in the fields alongside each other, they established bonds that linked family, community, and bright tobacco. In the process, they replaced the planter ideal with a new model that esteemed their own experiences. Unlike eighteenth- and nineteenth-century planters, who found social prestige in the domination of others and the management of their labor, twentieth-century farm families earned the respect of their neighbors in the demonstration of their own skills as farmers. Their work, they said, was not drudgery, but something with value and purpose far beyond the monetary return it might (but often failed to) produce. This new tobacco culture did not eradicate class biases, racism, and patriarchy, but it was inherently more democratic and egalitarian and ultimately provided farm families with a language they could use to articulate their own desires.

Before widespread mechanization in the second half of the twentieth century, bright tobacco farming revolved around a series of tasks that spanned the calendar. Preparations for a year's crop often began just as the previous year's crop was sold at market; many called it a "thirteen month crop." These preparations were culturally resonant. Farm families earned respect—from their neighbors, from warehousemen, and from tobacco buyers—by actually doing the work.

Throughout the late fall and early winter, families, often fathers and older sons, cut timber for the next year's curing fires. They might return to this job any time there was not pressing work. A 1930 study estimated that it took four acres of growing timber to supply enough wood to cure each acre of tobacco. Another expert reported that each curing could take two to three cords of dry wood, meaning that a family on a moderate-size tobacco farm might use dozens of cords during a season. Many did not actually cut the wood into small logs, preferring instead to push the felled trees into the fire as the curing progressed, but even so, cutting enough wood entailed a great deal of work. They also cut timber to make curing barns, which further accelerated deforestation throughout the Old Bright Belt, a problem that had grown worse by the 1920s.[4]

In the dead of winter, families prepared seedbeds where the tiny tobacco seeds could germinate before being transferred to the fields. It was intensive work, done usually on a southern exposure among the trees to resist freezing. After clearing and plowing a plot of ground, farmers burned leaves and forest debris to kill off weeds and grass and their seeds. They then applied fertilizers, scattered tobacco seeds, tramped on the ground, and covered the bed with pine boughs, canvas, or cheesecloth to protect the seedlings from the elements. Making a seedbed was usually men's work. Sallie Walker Stockard, a native of Alamance County, North Carolina, recalled her father taking his axe, mattock, hoe, and rake "deep into the woods" to make the seedbed. In 1922, Perry Miller, his twin brother Guy, his younger brother Ed, and two hired hands spent a combined eight days between January and March cutting out, plowing, burning, fertilizing, seeding, and covering a small seedbed on the farm of the Miller brothers' father. Since families rarely used the same seedbed twice, they repeated the same tasks every winter.[5]

While the seedlings grew to transplanting size, families prepared the fields. Farmers generally had their preferred spots for planting tobacco and often used them year after year. How they prepared the fields and the technologies they used changed over time. In the late nineteenth century, most plowed and fertilized the fields before dividing it into small hills where the plants would be set. By the early twentieth century, this last task was often skipped in favor of simply plowing the field into rows. Plowing took a great deal of strength and experience, so adult male farmers or their older sons usually worked the plow while younger sons carried and spread fertilizer. On the Miller farm, Perry and Guy, both twenty-two, did the majority of the plowing, while fourteen-year-old Edward did other tasks. Necessity often put women behind the plow, however.[6]

Transplanting began in May or even early June. It was tedious, backbreaking labor that involved digging the seedlings from the plant bed and carrying them to the fields and replanting them there. "Planting tobacco is about as tiresome [a job] as any man does," one Virginia farmer explained. "When night comes you are plum wore out, and your back feels broke." One man who grew up on a tobacco farm remembered how busy planting season was. "The whole family . . . took to the fields at planting time. Mama, who seldom worked outside the house, presided over the plantbed, pulling the plants carefully, and stacking them into the neat piles to be carried to the fields. There Papa took over, doing most of the planting himself. The smaller children dropped the plants, carefully placing one plant after another." While Sallie Walker Stockard, the daughter of a relatively prosperous white farmer, remembered "girls in calico bonnets, each with a basket on her arm, taking the plants to fields, dropping them one by one," Mabel Walthall, the seventeenth child of black sharecroppers, remembered the arduousness of the work. "You . . . had to bend over real low to stick the plant in the ground just right." Plants that did not take in the first transplanting had to be replaced with viable seedlings, a difficult task given the thousands of plants it took to cover even a small field.[7]

After planting, fields had to be constantly cultivated for several weeks to prevent weeds from overtaking the crops. Everyone strong enough to hold a hoe helped with this task until the plants grew large enough to shade the ground.

As they matured, the tobacco plants sprouted flowers in their terminal buds; the "topping" of the plants, removal of the flowers to concentrate growth in the leaves, was an important milestone in the year. Plants had to be topped just right so that each plant would have enough leaves to produce a large crop, but not so many that the quality of the plant's remaining leaves would suffer. Robert L. Ragland, who wrote widely about the cultivation of bright leaf to promote both the geographic expansion of the crop's growing area and sales of the seeds he produced on his Virginia farm, advised that the task of topping was so important that it "should be the work of experienced and trusty hands—men who can top, leaving any required number of leaves on a plant without counting."[8]

As Ragland's advice suggests, farm men often topped the plants. Topping was, in fact, one of several tasks throughout the seasons in which male tobacco farmers publicly demonstrated their skill in handling the crop. Improperly topped plants were a sign that a famer lacked skill or, worse, was lazy. The sight of plants "buttoning to blossom" or "fully blown," one writer asserted, was enough for some to "upbraid" a grower for "neglect."[9]

Suckering and worming followed topping in the tobacco farm family's calendar. Removing the terminal buds prompted the plants to sprout ancillary buds, commonly called suckers, underneath the leaves. Left unchecked, suckers could sap the leaves of nutrients, so farm families removed them by breaking them off. This had to be done very carefully to prevent damage to the plants. Older children were put to this important task, while the younger ones were sent with them to pick off tobacco hornworms.

Hornworms were just one of many pests tobacco growers encountered, but their rapacious appetites for the leaves, their untimely appearance in the summer growing season, and their general ugliness made them the farm family's special foe. "Some of the worms would be as big as your finger..." Mabel Walthall remembered, "and they would just sit on the end of their tails and they would click at you because they had horns, they were angry." Some families tried time-tested methods such as planting jimson weed in adjacent plots to draw the pests away from the tobacco or allowing domesticated turkeys to browse the fields for worms; others resorted to arsenic-based chemicals such as Paris Green. Most, however, relied on manual techniques. "One real nasty thing I had to do was worm tobacco," one woman remembered of growing up on the farm. "I could not pull the heads off of the big worms. Aunt Lillie gave me a jar and told me to put the worms in it, and she'd kill them at the end of the row."[10]

Tobacco farm children learned the intimacies of the crop while scouring the leaves of hornworms, oftentimes only a step or two behind their parents or older relatives. Hornworms have long featured in the stories tobacco farmers tell about their work and their lives. According to North Carolinian H. G. Jones, hands made green by tobacco sap and hornworm guts, stained so deeply that pumice-infused soap could not remove it, was the mark of tobacco farm kids. Virginian Lucille Payne felt that "your hands were always dirty, sticky, gooey."[11]

Summers brought other worries as well. In addition to hornworms, tobacco flea beetles, wireworms, cutworms, budworms, and white flies ate away at the plants. Hail was probably the cruelest enemy; it could cut the broad leaves to ribbons in mere minutes. A summer thunderstorm in 1925 destroyed the crops of nearly 150 farms in Vance County, North Carolina, making it necessary for the county Extension Service agent to seek the help of the Red Cross to secure enough garden crops to see the famers through the year. Granville wilt was nearly as fast and just as vicious. A bacterial disease that caused plant capillaries to clog and thus choke the plants, "the wilt" (as farmers called it) first appeared in Granville County, North Carolina, in 1880 and

Figure 2.1. Farm children often learned the tasks of worming and topping by their parents' sides. In Dorothea Lange's 1939 photograph of a Granville County sharecropper and his children, both sons and daughters scour the fields, including one child who is perhaps no more than two or three years old. Farm Security Administration/Office of War Information Photograph Collection, Library of Congress.

spread to adjoining regions. Reports of farm families seeing a diseased plant one day and losing the entire field overnight were not uncommon. Wildfire, frogeye, angular leafspot, black shank, and, beginning in the 1930s, blue mold could all ruin plants without warning. Until the chemical revolution of mid-twentieth century, farm families could do little to prevent these threats, and once they struck, families had little recourse. Disaster could often help bring neighbors together, though. If a family lost their crop early enough in the season, neighbors might share their extra seedlings; a family hit by hail could expect that their neighbors would help them salvage what was left of their crop.[12]

Harvesting season began as early as August and stretched into October. In some parts of the Old Bright Belt, families continued the older practice of cutting entire plants well into the twentieth century, but after the 1880s, the practice of priming—harvesting leaves individually as they ripened—slowly became universal. Priming made an already-pressing harvest season even more intense, since farm families had to return to their fields multiple times rather than harvesting the entire crop at once. It was, one observer put it, "much more troublesome" than the older practice of cutting. They also had to tie the leaves in bundles to sticks that could be suspended in the curing barns rather than simply nailing the plants to them, as they had done in earlier eras. And since raw leaves had to be cured within hours of picking, the decision to harvest a field required coordinated labor and concentrated effort. "The process of 'putting in' a barn of tobacco usually took a long day, and involved work by 10 or 15 people," remembered one native of Durham County, North Carolina.[13]

Because of its rigors, harvest time illustrated both the centrality of family labor and the social context within which it operated. With a looming pinch-point in the production process and a limited number of farm workers for hire, farm families, even relatively prosperous ones who might rely less on family workers in other seasons, turned to themselves to do the work. "The urgency of this crucial time demands every hand from the youngest child . . . to the oldest grandparent," explained sociologist Margaret Jarman Hagood of the harvests she witnessed on tenant farms in the 1930s.[14] Only the largest families could make it on their own; most swapped help with neighbors to get through the season. "Priming the tobacco, hauling it to the barn on sleds, tying the leaves to tobacco sticks and hanging the sticks in the barn, as well as the actual curing, often make it necessary to hire help or exchange labor with neighboring farmers," one observer noted.[15]

Even when contracts required sharecroppers to work on the farm of their landlord, landowner and cropper families interacted with one another in ways that sometimes belied the power relations that bound them together. Black men and white men worked together in the fields, and white women and black women worked side by side at the barns. Certainly the region's Jim Crow–era racial etiquette shaped these interactions—whites and blacks did not eat together, and black men no doubt approached white women with great care—but shared work experiences could muddy racial and class hierarchies, even if they did not challenge them. In 1939, photographer Dorothea Lange found three sharecropping families working together in ways that crossed lines of race, class, and gender. Mr. Taylor was a white sharecropper as was his neighbor Mr. Oakley, while Sam (as Lange identified him) was a black "share cropper and sub-tenant of Mr. Oakley." "Each of the three families supply workers and children to play around," she noted of their harvest work. "Of Taylor's family there are himself, his wife, young mother and baby, and his mother-in-law. Of Oakley's family there are himself, one-legged, his wife, a ten year old son, an eight year old daughter who kept care of Taylor's baby and two other younger children. Of the Negro family, there are Sam, a nearly grown son, a twelve year old son, and two or three younger children. This made sixteen of the families involved at the barns at one time or another in addition to two wage hands. There were eleven people working on one or another phase of 'putting in tobacco.'"[16]

Families usually divided the tasks of harvesting along lines of age and gender, although the latter division of labor could be quite permeable, especially for women. "From all other sorts of field work the mother takes off a half day or a day for the weekly washing and sometimes children are excused from field duty to help her," Hagood explained. Fathers usually had the final say. "Except where there is . . . a striving for social recognition which keeps daughters out of the field, or . . . enough sons so that daughters can be permanently assigned to household tasks, . . . father's claim for field work to take precedence over that of the mother. . . . By their crops they live and any less urgent matters can wait."[17]

In the fields, grown men and older boys picked leaves from the plants, working from the bottom of the plants to the top with each successive priming. Priming was backbreaking, especially in the first trips through the fields, when workers had to bend low through the thick upper leaves to reach those at the bottom. To prevent damage to leaves, primers carried them in their arms as they made their way to the harvesting sled that would convey them to the barns.

The relatively simple action of taking the leaves off the plant was further complicated by the fact that primers had to snap the leaves at the axil without damaging either the plants or the leaves. A damaged plant might not survive to be fully harvested; a damaged leaf might bring less money at auction. "My father would fuss if . . . you did not break the leaf close to the plant and catch most of the stem, or if, in handling it rough, you bruised or broke ribs on the leaf," Virginian William Hawthorne remembered of picking leaves in his youth. Learning to prime tobacco properly took years of experience. One World War II–era Extension Service agent's complaint that he was able to find plenty of "boys between the ages of 12 and 15 to help harvest tobacco" but few "experienced" workers "such as loopers and primers" in the face of looming labor shortages reveals much about the skill needed to harvest the crop. In fact, experienced primers could often make money on the side by helping farm families with fewer experienced hands. "A negro who lives in Henderson helps to recruit these workers and carries them with him to such farms as need this type of skilled tobacco primers," another Extension Service agent reported in 1943.[18]

Younger boys drove the harvested tobacco from the fields to the curing barns in small sleds (sometimes called slides or trucks) that were essentially wooden planks mounted on wooden runners; burlap sacks were arranged to make a four-sided bin on top. In this task, they learned the skills of handling the crops and the mules and the need to keep working without constant oversight. Driving sleds was, one woman recalled, "one of the more desirable tasks," but nevertheless it presented a number of challenges. "The paths they traveled over were always full of deep ruts in wet weather. Many truckloads of tobacco overturned in transit, creating [a] minor tragedy for the truckers and handers and, indirectly, to the whole crew in lost time and aggravation." Woe, too, to the boy who dawdled too long around the barns or stopped on the path to the fields when the men needed fresh sleds to fill.[19]

When the tobacco reached the barns, families prepared it for curing. Anyone not working in the fields could help string tobacco, but "this part of the labor was often done by the women of the family," one man recalled, "since it involved a little dexterity without too much back-bending labor." Farm women who stood all day in front of the wooden horses where they tied bundles of leaves to wooden sticks may have disagreed with his assessment of the difficulty of their work, but he was right about the nimbleness needed for the work. The work was tedious, and women had to be careful to tie the leaves tight; a loose leaf could land on the hot flues during the curing process and send an entire barn up in flames. Tying, sometimes called stringing or looping, was an art. After being handed a bunch of leaves, the stringer would "first station a knot on the end of the stick facing them and then . . . loop, a bunch at a time, on alternate sides of the stick until the stick was filled to the other end. There, the string was . . . tied in a knot and broken in two." Women prided themselves on their speed and recognized those who were especially skillful. Young girls learned the skill at the knees of their mothers, aunts, and older sisters. "We'd hand up tobacco leaves, three at a time, to be strung on a stick," one woman recalled of her childhood on the farm.[20]

After enough leaves had been picked and strung, the men came from the fields to hang the sticks on horizontal tier poles set at different heights inside the barns in order to get the curing process started. Young men climbed to the top of the barn using the tier poles as rungs and carefully hung the tobacco-laden sticks handed up by workers on the ground. . "Being big enough to straddle the tier poles . . . seemed to be somewhat of a status symbol among the young boys," one man recalled. "Climbing to the top of the barn . . . was even more of a sign of being a grown up [sic]."[21]

Once they finished filling the barn, families lit the curing fires. Adult male farmers usually oversaw the entire three-day process, but some families hired expert curers to make sure things went right. Part art, part science, curing techniques were idiosyncratic. Some farmers relied on curing "recipes" handed down for generations, but others, especially as bright tobacco agriculture spread in the late nineteenth century, continuously searched for just the right formula. Leading growers regularly offered their opinions in newspapers and pamphlets, while budding entrepreneurs sought to profit from their knowledge. Some, like the two men who charged farmers fifteen dollars for their secret recipe in 1891, were outright frauds. "Instead of curing bright," an editor explained of their formula, "it makes a nice black vapor."[22]

Families faced myriad challenges and dangers in curing. The heat, the timing, the humidity: all had to be watched carefully to ensure a proper curing. Fires, too, could easily rage out of control and burn a barn to the ground in minutes, so farmers slept lightly during the process. "With a bunk for a bed he stayed at the barn every night watching the fire," Sallie Walker Stockard recalled of her father. "All the sleep I got that fall was on the ground, lying around the tobacco barn, between spells of firing," Walter Corbett remembered of his first year as a farm owner. William Hawthorne's family had a portable shelter they could move from barn to barn since their curing barns were scattered across their land to ease the process of putting in a crop. "I would spend some nights there with my great uncle, who was the person responsible for seeing that the leaves turned out a golden flue-cured color," Shirley Underwood Troll wrote of growing up on a tobacco farm. "The fun part . . . was roasting potatoes and ears of corn in the fire used to cure the tobacco."[23]

Harvest time was indeed a time for cooking. Farm women moved between stringing in the barns and cooking in their kitchens during the harvest to see that the workers were all fed. The cooking continued with the curing. According to some traditions, Brunswick stew originated in Brunswick County, Virginia, in the 1820s. Whether it did is unclear, but Old Bright Belt families perfected numerous versions of the classic in their stewpots while tending the fires. More certain is the notion that the roots of North Carolina's unique barbecue styles are found in the long hours spent around the barns. One Caswell County, North Carolina, native remembered his father carefully basting the pork shoulder that cooked slowly as the tobacco cured, while he roasted corn, sweet potatoes and, once, his own foot in the ashes of the curing fire. "Sometimes all-night parties are held outside the barn around the furnace fire—with chicken stews, fiddle music, and story-telling," a writer for the North Carolina Writers' Project noted around 1940. "These are generally quiet affairs, designed to relieve the tedium of watching, and there is seldom any dancing or much merry-making. Livelier parties are often held at the end of the curing season." Salina McMillon remembered young men from the neighborhood showing up, guitars in hand, while her father and brothers cured tobacco. "Momma wouldn't allow us to go out there near them 'cause they was mean, but sometimes we would stand out and look at them and hear them." In their food and socializing, tobacco farm families made harvest time much more than a time for bringing the crops in. As families, extended kin, and even neighbors spent hours cooking, sharing local news and gossip, and playing music, they reinforced the linkages between family, community, work, and bright tobacco.[24]

Preparation of the tobacco for market followed curing. After the leaves were removed from the barn, they had to be stripped from the sticks and sorted by grade. Buyers bought leaves based on numerous qualities, including color and texture, and farmers did their best to sort their leaves based on these grades. Most had long boards divided by pegs into various grades on which they put leaves of similar quality together. Once they had three or four of the same grade, they tied them into bundles called hands. The hands served no purpose except to make the tobacco more attractive to sellers, but this was enough reason to make it a critical step in getting a crop ready for market.

The entire family helped strip and tie tobacco, but farm women often took control of it. "In the striphouse . . . the mother is often the star performer, the chief grader," wrote Hagood. "Although the husband does the directing, deciding what lots are to be worked next, assigns tasks to the children, he is usually somewhat respectful of his wife's ability." As with looping, some claimed that biology made women better at this task; women had better dexterity or more discerning eyesight or more patience, they said. "Men ain't no good in 'bacca," an older woman told Hagood. "They can't sit still and work steady. They's always got to be goin' outdoors to see about somp'n—even if they ain't got no excuse better'n the dog." The demands of the farm are the more likely reason. For male farmers, the end of tobacco harvesting meant the beginning of harvest season for other crops or the start of planting season for winter wheat. The time-consuming work of stripping and grading would pull them away from this work, while it was possible for women to combine grading with other tasks. "I'd grade tobacco all day long and pack it down," recalled one Stokes County, North Carolina, woman. "Then we'd tie it at night. You see, the pack house was right here at us, and the young 'uns could stay at the house." One woman Hagood interviewed could not grade, but she could tie, and she split the tasks with her husband. "She is proud of the fact that she can give her husband a two hours' start grading while she cleans the

Figure 2.2. In this 1939 photograph by Marion Post Wolcott, B. C. (Doc) Corbett, his wife, Nannie, and an unidentified son strip, sort, and tie tobacco for auction. The son is removing the tobacco from the sticks while his father sorts the tobacco by its various qualities. Nannie Corbett then tied the graded leaves into neat "hands" (visible by her feet) for the auction floor. Farm Security Administration/Office of War Information Photograph Collection, Library of Congress.

house and does all the cooking for the day, and still catch up with him in the early afternoon." Another woman did it so her husband could take a paying job after finishing the curing.[25]

Like harvest work, stripping and tying offered time for building bonds of family and community. "The work in the striphouse is favorable to conversation and tall tale telling," Hagood noted. One family she visited confessed to "telling 'mighty rough jokes'" as they stripped tobacco. "In several places a nephew, brother-in-law, grown son, or other relative was helping a man and his wife with stripping and the three were laughing or joking. . . . The cotton farm mother," she offered as comparison, "does not have such a good opportunity for combining sociability with work."[26]

Days, even weeks, of work in the strip house resulted in thousands of tightly packed hands of tobacco leaves, the tangible measure of a year's work. Farmers first made them to draw attention to the beauty of their crops, and the practice soon became the one of the several distinctive features of the bright tobacco auctions. Farm families packed them carefully for transport to market, where they displayed them with great skill, even artistically. Each hand, each leaf, was, in essence, their sweat, their knowledge, their skill put on display for neighbors to see and buyers to judge, so they took great pains to do it right. Those hands remained a cultural touchstone for farm families long after the practice of tying fell into disuse. They have even shown up, of all places, on license plates celebrating "Tobacco Heritage."[27]

When, in 1919, the Person County, North Carolina, Extension Service agent explained that "methods of raising tobacco have been handed down from father to son for several generations," he spoke of lessons learned during long hours in the fields and around the barns; of lessons learned with the legs and backs and hands; of lessons learned not only from fathers, but from mothers and uncles and aunts, too; of lessons not only in the mechanics of planting and cultivating and harvesting, but in the sight, the touch, and smell of good tobacco; of lessons, in short, in what it meant it to be a bright tobacco farmer. "After a man has 'fooled' with tobacco for a long time he will have a tobacco 'feel,'" Walter Corbett put it. By the early twentieth century, a new, unique tobacco culture had emerged from the old; farm families had made bright tobacco their own.[28]

3

Tobacco-Raising Fools

My bank account is in the bad;
My children are out of school;
My wife's clothing is very scant—
But I'm a tobacco-raising fool.
I go to the merchant to try for credit,
And always mortgage the mule;
It's ten to one I won't pay out—
But I'm a tobacco-raising fool.

EARL BOOTH (1924)

In the late nineteenth century, the promoters of bright tobacco made big promises about the crop. Prices were high, a Warren County, North Carolina, editor told his readers, because of "short supply" caused by the "enormous use that is being made of tobacco." Demand would never fall below supply, he counseled farmers in the pages of the *Gold Leaf*. "The prices may fall below what they are at now . . . but there will still be more money in growing a crop of tobacco than in making a crop of cotton."[1]

Sadly for farm families, he was wrong. Low prices were common in the half-century before the New Deal. The promising high prices of the 1870s faltered in the late 1880s, when increased production in eastern North Carolina and South Carolina put more leaf on the market and drove prices down. Prices fell precipitously in the 1890s, when the American Tobacco Company (ATC) gained near-monopoly power over much of the tobacco industry and farmers found fewer buyers for their crops. While the courts broke up the ATC in 1911, the resulting smaller companies did not create the competition necessary to drive prices up. Provisioning for World War I drove up demand

and prices, but both fell again after the war and bottomed out with the beginning of the Great Depression.

Low prices brought poverty to the Old Bright Belt, where almost everyone relied on tobacco to make a living. One Extension Service agent explained that the "majority of the farmers" in his county would "feel completely lost" without tobacco, but their attachment came at a high cost. "The entire county and all its farmers are now on the verge of bankruptcy," he reported in 1931 after three especially hard years. For many farm families, the Great Depression was only a variation on a theme. Some later remembered that the Depression years did not seem much harsher than any others.[2]

Poverty prompted repeated, almost continual protests in the Tobacco South generally, and the Old Bright Belt was no exception. Unlike wheat or corn or even cotton farmers, tobacco farmers did not dump their crops into anonymous global commodity markets but saw the leaves they grew enter factories just down the road from their farms and return to them with familiar names like Lucky Strike or Chesterfield. To a farmer paying hefty warehouse fees to sell a crop for a pittance to companies making millions of dollars a year, there was no need to blame faraway bankers, lawyers, and railroads for his plight: he knew the names and addresses of those who profited handsomely from his and his family's labor.

Channeling farmers' anger into constructive reforms was another matter, however. Farmers joined a string of organizations chartered to alleviate their condition. Some, such as the Farmers' Alliance, were tied to larger rural protests, while others were homegrown. Whatever the scale of these organizations, farm families saw in them the opportunity to challenge the power over the auctions held by warehousemen and tobacco companies. As farm families joined them, they brought an emerging culture of family-based tobacco agriculture, in which families asserted their own notions of quality, value, and worth rooted in their work experiences, and they voiced their plight as people who worked with neighbors and kin. Their organizations reflected this egalitarian culture and argued that small farmers should be able to make a living as well as large ones, that markets should be fairer and more transparent, that their own expertise should be recognized and cultivated, and that farmers should cooperate with each other for the betterment of all.

All of the organizations farmers created failed to achieve these reforms, for numerous reasons. The ideas they promoted and the ideals they voiced were more resilient, however. When we view them as part of a long protest tradition rather than as discrete phenomena, it becomes clear that the numerous protest organizations that swept through the Old Bright Belt in the years between Reconstruction and World War I offered farm families the tools to refine their vision of tobacco agriculture as a family-centered enterprise. They also prepared them to advocate for policies that would defend this vision.

The loose leaf auction system of selling tobacco had its roots in nineteenth-century Danville, Virginia. Beginning 1730, Virginia law required that all tobacco be prized, or pressed into hogshead barrels, and inspected before sale to Great Britain. (Inspectors drilled a hole in each barrel and pulled out a sample to inspect the tobacco.) As tobacco agriculture spread into the Piedmont in the late eighteenth century, new inspection stations followed so planters would not have to travel to Richmond or Petersburg to sell their crops. The station at Danville, which was established in the 1790s, quickly became popular; it took in crops not only from southern Virginia but from adjoining regions of North Carolina as well. In the early nineteenth century, buyers and sellers alike chafed under the inspection system and its prizing requirements, and over time sales of loose tobacco to domestic manufacturers increased. In Danville, by the 1850s, the growing popularity of bright tobacco had reinforced buyers' desire to be able to see the crops and the sale of loose-leaf tobacco had become common. By the 1870s, the weakening and near-abandonment of Virginia's inspection laws had established the loose-leaf auction as the sole method for selling bright tobacco there. Millions of pounds of loose tobacco passed over Danville's sales floors in the late nineteenth century—more than 40 million pounds a year on average by the 1890s. Millions more pounds passed from farm families to the tobacco trade in warehouses that popped up in towns throughout the Old Bright Belt as bright tobacco agriculture expanded geographically.[3]

No one who visited an Old Bright Belt tobacco warehouse on auction day left unimpressed. Auction warehouses, large brick buildings with broad sales floors, were both unadorned and imposing. Every market town had several warehouses. Although each vied for farmers' business by promising the best conditions or the best rates or the best buyers, sales were handled identically on every floor. Nevertheless, farmers usually had their favorite warehouses where they liked to sell. On auction day, farmers of all statuses arrived at the warehouse, their wagons (and later, trucks and cars) loaded down with the hands of tobacco they had so carefully tied in preparation for sale. After unloading and weighing it for sale, black warehouse workers called truckers lined up the tobacco baskets in neat, tight rows on the warehouse floors. As they waited for the auction to start, sellers talked about the market or bought a bite to eat at the snack bar, anything to pass the time as they waited to see what a year's labor would bring. "When markets open in the Old Bright Belt," one observer explained, "it seems that every breath is held in suspense until the first sale is chanted by the auctioneer."[4]

By all accounts, the auction was a spectacle, the auctioneer its star. "He starts off in a whoop and holds out remarkably well, uttering not a single word that is audible to an unpracticed ear," observed writer A. B. Bradsher. As he moved through the piles, "he solicits bids," another observer noted, "using his tongue, his hands, and his body to the best advantage. His jargon is unintelligible to all but the initiated." Artist Clare Leighton saw in the auctioneer's spasms and rhythmic chant a "medicine man." "He sways and dances, in an ecstatic swoon, the strangest combination of rhythm and vulgarity. In appearance he is like a tout at the races, and against the grace of the Negro porter and packer he has additional coarseness. Yet there is about him the inevitable beauty of complete abandon." In full control of the action, he nevertheless appeared "so drunk with self-created excitement that unconsciously he half closes his eyes as he waves his hands around and points and shakes throughout his entire body. There is no peripheral rhythm; this comes from the core of the man." A tobacco auctioneer she interviewed put it more simply: "When I'm feeling good . . . you can hear me across the warehouse." Some estimated that auctioneers could sell nearly 600 piles per hour, but most markets limited them to 360 per hour, or a pile every ten seconds.[5]

As the auctioneer rattled off prices, the buyers picked at the piles, pulling out samples to see, smell, and feel. Every sale had buyers of several types. The biggest buyers were the ones from the major U.S. and British tobacco companies; they usually sought out specific qualities in the leaves that matched the products their employers made. Independent leaf dealers purchased tobacco for resale later to specialized or non-U.S. manufacturers who did not have buyers on the market or to the big cigarette makers when they needed additional leaf.

Alongside these more established buyers were speculators, commonly known by the derisive term pinhookers, who specialized in buying less desirable lots of tobacco for a low price, reorganizing them, and then reselling them for a profit. Pinhookers in Danville, one observer noted, were "veritable hawks" who could quickly "pluck fifty dollars" from a farmer "by buying his tobacco and selling it right before him." Farmers disliked pinhookers immensely, not only because they made their profits from the farmers' work but also because their ability to play the market reminded farmers of their own vulnerability to its vagaries. Farmers had to stand by as these men, some of them complete strangers, judged the value of their work in front of anyone who cared to look.[6]

Farmers thus had mixed feelings about the auctioneers and the sales they directed. The auction system offered some benefits. For one, warehousemen cut checks payable at local banks as soon as the auctions ended, so families, even many tenants, could walk away with cash in hand. Prices were also locally competitive, not set by distant commodity markets. Prices also reflected the quality of the leaves, not just aggregate supply. This meant that with a desirable lot of tobacco, any farmer could make a decent profit if the buyers wanted to compete for it. Most appreciated the freewheeling atmosphere; no one knew what a given lot of tobacco could bring, and many relished the gamble. In a good year, the sight of the auctioneer "bidding up" the crops created palpable excitement and seemed to confirm the promise that bright tobacco paid better than cotton ever would. Even in a bad year, farmers could still hope that their best leaves might catch the buyers' attention. One scholar notes that at the Great Depression's deepest moment, when average tobacco was bringing barely a dime a pound, "farmers look on hopefully rather enjoying the annual show."[7]

For many, selling tobacco was as much a family affair as growing and curing it was. Margaret Jarman Hagood noted that some white tenant farm mothers paid as close attention to the market as their husbands; some even paid closer attention. "Their knowledge of farming matters is surprising and pertains not only to the immediate condition of the current crop but to details of renting, credit . . . and to the basic data for making an estimate of how they will 'come out this year.'"[8]

It was common for farm wives and children to have a portion of the crop they could call their own. When Sam J. Hite of Lunenburg County, Virginia, came to the market at South Hill in 1929, his son and two daughters came along to sell their portions too. The father and son sold a combined six lots, as did the sisters. "Misses Bettie and Helen's six lots ranged from 22 ½ to 46, bringing them an all around price of $31.05," the local newspaper noted. "The young ladies claim they did all the work except, of course, the plowing." One twelve-year-old Virginia boy told of how, when his mother died, he received from his father "1,000 hills of tobacco to buy my clothing with."[9]

Hagood pointed out the practical limits of dividing the crop among family members. One family she interviewed had allotted portions of the crop to the mother, who got "all except the landlord's fourth from her tobacco patch," from which she was "supposed to buy her own and her younger children's clothes," and to the "three older boys," who were "allowed the proceeds of a patch, which they [were] to share with the two older sisters for cooking and keeping house and especially for taking care of their bird dog, their most prized possession." Hard times, however, had thwarted these plans. All of the mother's money had gone instead for the burying of a child and the down payment on a new stove, while the fertilizer and grocery bills had taken more than the share the father allotted for himself, forcing him to take from the children's shares. "He took enough to finish paying his debt at the store and

Figure 3.1. Entire families often came to the market to sell their tobacco and experience the auctions. In Marion Post Wolcott's 1939 photograph, Elvin and Rosa Wilkins debate whether to accept the bid on their tobacco or "turn the tag" and try their luck elsewhere. They ultimately agreed to accept the price. Farm Security Administration/Office of War Information Photograph Collection, Library of Congress.

Figure 3.2. Her family's tobacco sold, Rosa Wilkins used the trip to town as an opportunity to buy both necessities and luxuries that had been deferred until the fall. Farm Security Administration/Office of War Information Photograph Collection, Library of Congress.

let them have the remainder without keeping back any money to run on for the year."[10]

Auctions meant a trip to town for rural people, and farm families used it as an occasion to shop and socialize as they sold their crops. Shop owners held sales and decorated their windows to entice farm families to spend their tobacco money. Salesmen of all sorts populated the street corners outside the auction houses, hawking patent medicines, shoes, livestock, and any number of other items. Street preachers jostled with them for space. Before cars and trucks made travel to markets easier, many male farmers would camp overnight in the racially segregated bunk rooms that warehouses provided. At loose ends and bored, farmers would hang out on street corners listening to itinerant musicians, test their aim in makeshift shooting galleries, or socialize in cafes and pool halls. Some sought other, illicit pleasures. Bootleggers and prostitutes found plenty of business during marketing season and sometimes traveled from market to market as the calendar dictated.

Figure 3.3. Salesmen of all sorts pulled out all the stops to entice both white and black buyers at the auctions. Here a patent medicine salesman hawks his wares outside a Durham tobacco warehouse. Farm Security Administration/Office of War Information Photograph Collection, Library of Congress.

Because of this atmosphere, some debated the propriety of women coming to the auctions. Nevada Jane Hall, a white woman from Stokes County, North Carolina, "never went to the tobacco market when her father took the crop to be sold, because women who went to the market were considered huzzies." Salina McMillon, a black woman from Granville County, North Carolina, similarly remembered riding to town with her father and brothers, but never going to the warehouse. "I'd come with my father bringing the tobacco in to auction in Durham, and sometimes in Oxford," she told an interviewer, but she "didn't go down to the warehouse with all those folks—he wouldn't let me." In fact, she admitted, "I didn't want to be down there where a crowd of mens were." Still, many grown women stood on the auction floors as their crops were sold. "You know, I love to go the market!" an elderly Lillie Tart remembered of the years she and her sisters raised and sold tobacco alongside their mother.[11]

Even as they enticed farm families, auctions also alienated them. "It is easy to distinguish the farmers from the buyers," sociologist T. J. Woofter noted. "The former are in 'town' clothes and look uncertain. The latter are well dressed and assured." Rural reformer Archie Swanson Beverley gave voice to the minor humiliations farm families endured in a parable in which a farmer complains of the "buyers, dealers, and pinhookers who passed judgment on the quality of our schoolin', our roads, and our homes." The entire auction scene only added insult to pain farm families felt when they saw their year's labor "knocked out" for a pittance. "Many's the time," Beverley's protagonist admitted, "I've come back home to Sarah with tears in my eyes—and 'chicken feed' in my pocket." Even leading planter Robert L. Ragland could sympathize with the average farm family's frustration. "Go into these modern tobacco marts and see the number of warehousemen, weighers, auctioneers, clerks, canvassers, laborers and retainers[,] every one of whom are paid far more for handling planters' tobacco than those who raise it! What wonder, then, that [he] . . . goes home disappointed, dissatisfied, and dejected."[12]

Warehousemen, buyers, and other elites, including large planters, regularly blamed farm families for their own plight. They accused farming people of improvidence and bad management. Pittsylvania County, Virginia, planter William T. Sutherlin accused common farmers of a litany of failures, including not growing enough foodstuff, not raising livestock, taking out too much credit, and failing to live frugally. "Will he and his family agree to wear old clothes and stop buying everything except the actual necessities of life?" he asked of the region's small farmers. "Will he pledge himself to stop running around to all the country stores within his reach, and to remain at home and attend to his own business until he is able to pay his debts and buy for cash?" Just as often, elites offered blanket indictments of farm families and criticized their lack of skill. "It has been explained time and again and yet it bears repetition," one editor wrote. "Make preparations for a full crop of all home supplies and then lay off as many acres of your best tobacco land as can be well and properly cultivated. Devote what time you can give to tobacco to growing only the best and brightest. No other will pay you this year." "Over production and the poor quality of the crops have combined to depress the markets everywhere," another editor argued, similarly suggesting that families planted more tobacco than they could give proper attention to and thus were to blame for low prices. "Farmers must learn . . . that it will not pay to make sorry tobacco," another warned. "It is *quality* not *quantity* that pays."[13]

When Sutherlin blamed "the cry of 'hard times'" on the "habit of many land-owners . . . to entrust the cultivation of their farms to ignorant and un-skilled tenants who make nothing but common tobacco," he revealed a deep distrust not just for tenants, especially African Americans, but also for the labor system that put families in charge of their own work. Others echoed this sentiment. Philip Alexander Bruce blamed the absence of planters who could "enforce [a] degree of discipline." "Tobacco requires the most thor-ough information and the most discriminating skill," he noted, adding that slaves "were specially educated from childhood to do general or special work and . . . attained . . . much expertness in the various tasks of the barns and fields." "But under the present system," he concluded, "this is impossible and the result is that labor of the new regime is generally inferior in character." Complaints about the skill and motivation of tenants continued well into the twentieth century. "It is this tenant system that is running down so many farms in the South to-day," pronounced one Mecklenburg County, North Carolina, planter in 1905. A generation later, author Roy C. Flannagan heard much the same from elites. "Unskilled tenants, no matter how intelligent, rarely can raise leaf that will bring a price above the cost of production."[14]

When they were not denigrating the ability of farming families to handle tobacco, elites accused them of not using the latest techniques. One editor upbraided Old Bright Belt growers about the higher yields growers in east-ern North Carolina were getting. "Why is this?" he asked. "Is it not that our planters . . . stick to the old methods of cultivation and curing while the planters down east . . . test all modern appliances to their satisfaction, hence get the latest improvements in the line of implements, barns &c? Watch out. Don't let the old rut hold you in its course to your detriment." The president of the Danville Tobacco Association chided farm families for continuing to use older methods of cutting the whole plant at harvest instead of priming and curing the leaves separately, as New Belt growers were doing. "Trade a type of tobacco that is needed for which they are always willing to pay a good price."[15]

The condescension of elites followed common farmers to the auction floors. Suggestions that farm families stole money from their own pockets by not grading their tobacco properly could sound like blame-fixing. "The *Gold Leaf* has repeatedly urged upon farmers the importance of carefully assorting their tobacco before carrying it to market," one editor chided, warning farm-ers not to "entrust [grading] to negroes or inexperienced hands" but instead "to overlook the assorting yourself or have some competent person to do it."

Another offered a story of a pinhooker who purchased a lot of tobacco from a farmer for $9 per hundred pounds and sold it for an average of $12.50 per hundred after sorting it better. "That's an example of how the planter treats himself," the editor concluded, "and yet he goes off and does the same thing again."[16]

Casting low prices and poverty as the result of some failing on the part of farm families—saying they grew too much tobacco, grew poor tobacco, failed to market it properly, or just didn't economize enough—elites held the market structures that were the more likely culprits blameless. The most fundamental of these structures was a limited number of buyers in relation to the number of sellers at any given auction. Hoping to attract sellers to their floors, warehousemen touted the quality of the buyers they attracted. "We have the location, the best facilities for receiving, shipping, and handling leaf tobacco," the owners of Cooper's Warehouse in Henderson, North Carolina, bragged, "and above all, we have the largest, wealthiest, strongest and most liberal corps of dealers in the State, and are determined to have your tobacco if money and liberal prices will get it." Even in the busiest towns, however, only a dozen or so buyers, not all of whom were in the market for the same types of leaves, might be on the floor. Smaller towns had even fewer. If a seller came on the wrong day, the results could be disastrous. "I took a little tobacco to the market a few days ago & sold it for nothing scarcely, hardly enough to pay for the guano that was put under it ($2 ½)," tenant J. E. Bennett wrote to his landlord in the midst of harvest season in 1886. "They say they, nor the buyers, don't want any tobacco just yet. Say they can't tell what they have on hand yet."[17]

Even when competing with one another over a pile of tobacco, manufacturers and (to a lesser extent) speculators, benefited from the mismatch between supply and demand, a feature of the tobacco market that kept prices low. Beginning in the 1890s, manufacturers perfected methods for redrying and storing tobacco almost indefinitely. The ATC and others adopted policies of keeping roughly three years' worth of tobacco on hand as a hedge against shortages. This meant that that they did not *have* to buy tobacco at auction in any given year. They could wait, while farmers most definitely could not. Growers, Woofter put it simply, were "in a buyers' market."[18]

Credit arrangements, including the crop lien, meant that many farmers, especially tenants, had to sell their crops before their contracts expired. By the beginning of the twentieth century, the marketing season, which had once stretched well into the following year, had collapsed into a mad rush to get crops on the auction floor as early as possible. "The farmers of the Old Bright Belt . . . cannot hold the bulk of their crop until after Christmas," the president of the Danville Tobacco Association explained in 1927 when he requested that buyers hold additional sales to meet the needs of sellers. Tenants feared that having the "bulk of their crop in the packinghouses ungraded" would give landlords "a very decided advantage in dictating terms for the coming year." "Possibly 50 to 75% of both landlords and tenants," he continued, relied on credit for just about everything during the year and needed to settle their debts quickly at harvest. "You let October, November and December come and go and the farmer who has taken no steps or few steps to liquidate his obligations will find his credit gone," he explained. With so many sellers on the market, buyers felt no pressure to bid high, even on the best tobacco. "Thus it becomes a game among the buyers," Woofter remarked, "not to bid on the merits of each lot of tobacco, but to secure their requirements at as low a price as possible, figuring always on the supply coming into the market rather than the demand."[19]

Farm families described this phenomenon in conspiratorial terms, accusing buyers of distorting the market through collusion and other means. In 1911, farmers in Vance County, North Carolina, accused tobacco buyers of spreading inflated estimates of the size of the tobacco acreage in order to drive prices down. "In the face of such dishonesty do you wonder why we poor farmers sometimes get up in the back?" they pleaded. At harvest, another farmer claimed, the farmer has "to drop everything . . . hire all the labor he can pay for . . . to save it and get it cured and ordered to sell before the market shuts down. If he don't, first thing he knows them buyers'll holler 'overproduction' and cut the prices." While no one ever accused tobacco buyers of saintly behavior—Woofter alleged that they paid more for the crops of large growers and that "poor unknowns" had "to make up for that"—they had no real reason to practice widespread fraud. According to Woofter, "actual collusion in fixing bidding limits is hardly necessary—a gentleman's agreement not to 'hog the market' would seem to be ample enough."[20]

Growers' only hope was that manufacturers' stock of certain types of leaves were short. Black tenant farmer Arthur Barnes bragged that it "always seemed that I had pull with the leading men. If I had a grade of tobacco Colonel Matthews of the Imperial [Tobacco Company, the main British buyer] could use, I'd call him; he'd look out for me." Most farmers had no such access, though. Buyers never publicly announced what types of leaves they preferred for making their proprietary blends, much less how much of these different leaves they might have on hand. Farmers often complained about the mystifying and secret grading scales buyers used, and they felt insulted when buyers downgraded leaves they had spent so much time grading and packing. Seeing a pinhooker buy a pile the company buyers had deemed trash, rearrange it, and sell it for a higher price only heightened their resentment.[21]

Even if growers knew what buyers wanted, they likely would not have had the ability to translate that knowledge to the fields or packing houses. In the nineteenth century, the language of grading reflected the mixture of manufacturing uses (cutters, fillers, wrappers, smokers), empirical descriptions (yellow, red, bright, waxy, fine), plant location and cultural descriptions (lugs, primings), and judgment calls (common, good, fancy) that buyers considered when buying leaf. "A good wrapper leaf in a pile of fillers is lost. Don't get cutters and wrappers mixed with each other. Don't mix smokers and fillers, or in short be sure not to let one grade into another grade," the editor of the *Gold Leaf* exhorted in 1888, illustrating only a brief range of the variables. It was a confusing system but a relatively open one that farmers could intuit with experience.[22]

Increasing demand for bright tobacco for cigarette manufacturing in the years before World War I changed the language of the market. Older terms remained common among farmers but became less precise descriptors of the measures manufacturers were using when buying leaf. A farm family could arrange their tobacco based on one quality, only to find that that was not at all the quality buyers were using when judging its worth. Assurances by the president of the Danville Tobacco Association that a "not too heavy bodied bright tobacco would not fail to sell well" were hardly enlightening. Even the U.S. Department of Agriculture's Extension Service, which used federal, state, and local dollars to put agricultural experts in counties across the United States (including every Old Bright Belt county), could offer only weak suggestions that growers sort their leaves better. Tobacco companies had little reason to share their grades—one dealer said the ATC had more than a hundred of them by the late 1920s—because they benefited from farm families' lack of information.[23]

The structural disadvantage of farmers drove movements to remake the auction system. Farm leaders first voiced calls to organize themselves to challenge the power of warehousemen and manufacturers in the 1870s, and they repeated them almost constantly in the half-century before the New Deal. In response, farm families moved through a series of organizations in the hope of effecting meaningful change.

The Patrons of Husbandry, better known as the Grange, came first. Founded in 1868, the Grange movement established itself in Virginia and North Carolina in 1872 and then swept through both states in the wake of the Panic of 1873. At its peak in 1875, the organization claimed more than 24,000 members in the two states, many of them in the Old Bright Belt counties around Danville. Large Old Bright Belt growers, including planters William T. Sutherlin and Robert L. Ragland, took leadership roles in the Grange, and most local leaders were men of some standing. Little is known about rank-and-file Grangers in the Old Bright Belt, but the organization's program of reform reflected an elite perspective on the problems tobacco farmers faced. The main points of the platform were that warehousemen charged unjustifiably high prices, committed fraud by speculating in the tobacco they sold, and sought the appointment of corrupt inspectors who were willing to take larger-than-normal samples so the warehousemen could resell it."[24]

To correct these problems, Grangers pressed warehousemen to lower their fees and asked the Virginia legislature to strengthen the state inspection system. Grangers had no great love for the inspection system as it was, but they desired to retain the inspectors' function as a "neutral" mediator "between buyer and seller." When warehousemen tried to shirk inspection entirely by using a loophole in the law that allowed private houses to sell tobacco without inspection, the Grangers called for state ownership of auction warehouses. When this approach proved unfruitful, the Grangers opened their own warehouse in Danville in 1876. Although the venture ultimately failed in 1879, it pushed warehousemen in Danville to lower their fees. Satisfied for a time, farmers dropped their protests and Grange membership in Virginia and North Carolina declined.[25]

Despite its ultimate failure in the Piedmont, the Grange movement established a two-pronged model for organizing Old Bright Belt farm families that inspired later organizations. First, while the National Grange spoke of predatory railroads and unscrupulous bankers, Old Bright Belt Grangers talked tobacco. Virginia Grange master Dr. J. M. Blanton captured the strength of this interest well in his 1877 address to the state convention. He compared the "soulless corporations . . . known as railroads" with the "probably just as soulless" tobacco boards of trade.[26]

Just talking about the tobacco market was not enough to build support, of course, so the Grangers also articulated a vision for fixing it that reflected the vision of Old Bright Belt farmers of themselves and their needs. Tobacco families built their identities in relation to the crop. They defended their skill and ability to manage their crops and merged a stubborn faith in their abilities with producerist notions of the value of their labor. They had the right to the full value of these, they argued. As Robert L. Ragland put it in his support of state-owned warehouses, they had "vested rights" that the state ought to defend from unscrupulous inspectors and warehousemen who would rob them. Grangers across the Old Bright Belt concurred and sent petitions in support of Ragland's bill to create public warehouses. This rhetoric outlived the Grange: in fact, it grew stronger as more farm families became more active in the actual work of growing bright tobacco.[27]

The second key to the Grange's relative success was its use of existing community networks to build support. Following the model of the National Grange, orators and leaders talked to farmers gathered at schools, churches, and crossroads stores and at the meetings of other agricultural associations, encouraging them to join the organization, often with great success. By 1875, there were at least nine locals in Pittsylvania County alone. Master John J. Wilkinson established six of them, as well as one in neighboring Henry County, Virginia, in the span a few months.[28]

Meetings of the locals, which were closed to nonmembers, were akin to religious revivals and reflected the national organization's advocacy of "organization, education, and co-operation." Grangers discussed business, listened to speakers, and sang songs to encourage one another and build a sense of shared commitment. One Mecklenburg County newspaper editor reported hearing the "vocal exercises" of the Chase City Grange from outside the hall where they met. At a meeting of the Williesburg Grange in Charlotte County, Virginia, the "brethren and sisters" enjoyed "a splendid barbecue, worthy of ancient times" before adjourning to the local Presbyterian church, where the Grand Lecturer of the state Grange "urged the farmers to come forward, and in the bonds of brotherly love assist each other in the battle for life."[29]

Male Grangers encouraged farm women to join them. "If the great agricultural interest of the State is to be carried successfully over the tempestuous ocean over which it is now tossed, we must have the *intelligent* sympathy and co-operation of woman—*she* must guide the helm," the Virginia State Grange proclaimed in 1874. Girls over the age of sixteen were eligible for membership, and a strong contingent of women kept most locals functioning. Locals also had offices for women, but they held little power. Each local had a Lady Steward who oversaw the work of female Grangers, but the other three offices were honorific. Called Ceres, Flora, and Pomona after the classical goddesses of agriculture, the offices reflected leaders' assumption that the "presence of woman will give the Order virtue, dignity, and character." The women holding them sat in special seats where they oversaw the meetings as symbols of the goddesses and did little else.[30]

Women's offices in the Grange illustrated how elite men idealized white women's farm work. These women, Grange leaders assumed, might grow flowers or even vegetables but did not do true farm work, which was better left to white and black men and black women. One Granger justified opening membership to women on the grounds that "thousands of widows" needed "the active co-operation and assistance of man" to protect them from the "agents and middlemen" who oversaw their farms and "worked assiduously to accumulate for themselves at the expense of their employers." Virginia Grange leaders felt that in the aftermath of the Civil War the organization could in fact protect white women from having to do manual labor. "If in life, and prepared for the new field in the wreck and ruin which have been brought upon us by the results of the war, the change from wealth to poverty, from slave to free society, our lovely and refined women are to be saved from the position of menials, *they* must not be forgotten in effort to ameliorate the condition of our class. . . . Let it not be said we have taken woman out her proper sphere and will sap the foundations of society." This conception of farm women's interests revealed the class biases of the Granger leadership not only in the Old Bright Belt but throughout the South generally. Grange leaders could not conceive that elite white women would willingly doing manual labor, including farm work and did not feel that non-elite white women were worthy of their protection.[31]

These prejudices extended to black men and women as well. The Grange extended membership to whites only. Speeches and writings by leading Grangers evince no concern over the plight of black farmers and often lamented that emancipation had occurred. Committed to white supremacy and the Democratic Party, many disdained the political power black men might wield and therefore did nothing to cultivate it.

While Piedmont Grangers no doubt voiced the same the complaints as small landowners and landless farmers, their elitism and racism undercut the organization's ability to create a broad-based reform movement. Deep class divisions separated whites in the Old Bright Belt. During the Civil War, the region, especially North Carolina, had been a hotbed for Unionists who resented the elites who they felt had pushed secession. Heated battles between conservative Democrats and Republicans continued into the postwar years. Political violence in Alamance and Caswell Counties in that state grew so intense that Governor William Holden declared martial law in 1870 to suppress Ku Klux Klan assaults on and murders of black and white Republicans. For more than a decade after that, Republicans and Democrats on both the Virginia and North Carolina sides of the Old Bright Belt challenged each other at the polls (and away from them, too).

Political divisions hamstrung reform efforts after the Grange's popularity waned in the late 1870s. In Virginia, state tobacco inspection was a volatile issue, and support and opposition to it mapped imperfectly to party affiliation. Conservative Funders, Democrats who argued Virginia should pay its antebellum debt completely (many of whom were warehousemen and their allies), opposed continuing state inspections, while Readjusters, a coalition of black and white Republicans and dissident Democrats (many of whom were small farmers) who said the debt should be readjusted to reflect the state's changed situation, pushed to strengthen inspection. When the Readjusters swept to power in 1879, Funders—many of whom had benefited from the graft of traditional inspection and had no interest in continuing state inspection with neutral inspectors—jumped at the opportunity to lambaste the system as an opportunity for political cronyism.

In October 1883, Danville's leading Funders, a group that included most of the leading warehousemen and tobacco manufacturers, accused the city's Readjuster leadership of destroying the town's burgeoning tobacco trade by driving away from the "hundreds" of North Carolina farmers who "used to sell their tobacco in our market" but "now go five times as far to market in their own State, *on account of the negro rule in our town.*"[32] Funders also complained that Readjuster leaders said they "did not want the people of North Carolina to come here anyway." While the charge was entirely untrue—one Funder admitted later that the claim was "extreme in language and hasty in construction"—the dispute over tobacco market was, according to one witness, one of several factors that fueled tension in the weeks before the town's infamous 1883 "riot" that left several black men dead and opened the door for the Democrats to overthrow the Readjusters at the polls.[33]

This political climate made the post-Reconstruction years an inauspicious time for building biracial coalitions. The leaders of the Knights of Labor learned this painful lesson when the organization sought to organize tobacco farmers after the decline of the Grange movement. The Knights of Labor, which was founded with the goal of organizing all laborers, offered membership to farmers of all classes, from landowners to farm workers, all races, and all genders. Like the Grange, the Knights employed lecturers and organizers who met engaged rural people at country stores, church services, and other gatherings to talk up the benefits of organizing. In the mid-1880s, a number of locals sprang up across the Old Bright Belt, mostly in North Carolina. Railroad and factory workers accounted for the membership of most of the locals, but farmers and farm workers made up the majority of members in a few locals. In rural Caswell County, North Carolina, farm hands, washerwomen, cooks, and farmers created a local in the small community of Pelham. Rural Rockingham and Person Counties also had a few locals with similar membership.[34]

The Knights of Labor was especially successful in recruiting black workers and farmers. Comparatively few whites, especially white farmers, joined. Organizers rightly assessed that a combination of racism and social stigma kept white farmers away. "The colored people have an organizer, and a very worthy and efficient one," a Knights leader wrote from Durham in 1886, "and while [he] will be a useful worker among the colored people, he is utterly useless to us among the whites." A Virginia leader expressed similar reservations that same year. "I have notices from three . . . Counties to organize White assemblies. . . . I hope you do not expect these white assemblies to be organized by a Colored Organizer." The following year, a leader in Oxford, North Carolina, complained that local Democrats reviled white Knights for their involvement with the organization. "The Assemblies of this place and vicinity wish me to make known . . . the unenviable position of the Knights of Labor here. As soon as it became generally known that we had an Assembly here persecution followed, and no stone was left unturned to create ill-feeling against us. . . . They pointed at us with scorn and kept crying 'Nigger! Nigger!' until the two words 'Nigger' and 'Knights' became synonymous terms."[35]

Racism was not the only factor that hindered the Knights' attempts to organize Old Bright Belt farm families. Many white farmers recoiled at the organization's seeming radicalism. Although the founding principles of the Knights hearkened back to the producerist republicanism of the early republic, many thought its goals were radical. The explosion of a bomb at Chicago's Haymarket Square during a strike by the Knights in May 1886 opened the door for the organization's enemies to associate it with the anarchists who were ultimately charged with the crime. Workers across the country distanced themselves from the organization almost overnight. In the Old Bright Belt, organizers bemoaned the unfortunate connection as another impediment to their work.

Even without this association with radicalism, the Knights' appeals would not likely have resonated among Old Bright Belt growers. Larger landowners tended to see themselves as managers, not workers, and believed themselves to have little in common with the workers they hired. They likely would have reacted with horror had their sharecroppers organized. Small landowning farm families and even many tenants, the groups the Knights really hoped to draw in, did not conceive of themselves as workers in the way the Knights hoped. While they may have sympathized with many of the Knights' producerist ideas, they did not feel alienated from the means of production or the fruits of their labor. Indeed, their work in the soil and among the leaves made them feel more connected to them, not less. It was only when they carried those leaves to the auction floor that they felt powerless.

This is why any group hoping to organize Old Bright Belt farmers and their families needed to do more than motivate them with fine sermons on rural cooperation; they also needed to talk about ways of improving the tobacco market. While the Knights opened a tobacco factory in Raleigh with the goal of making and selling their own tobacco, it never confronted the problem of the auction. This was a strategic error that cost the group any opportunity it may have had to extend its reach into the fields.

The Southern Farmers' Alliance successfully fused the need for rural cooperation and the need for a restructuring of the tobacco marketing system for a time in the late 1880s and early 1890s, just as the American Tobacco Company was strengthening its stranglehold on the auctions. Founded in Texas, the Alliance swept across the South in the late 1880s. Its goal, as articulated by its most influential leader, Charles Macune, was to organize farmers as a way of challenging the industrial capitalism of the day. While its rhetoric drew heavily on Jeffersonian republicanism and its organizers relied heavily on local and neighborhood networks tied to churches and schools, the Alliance pushed farmers to become more modern, more businesslike. Across the South, farmers who were fearful of losing their land because of low prices for cotton and tobacco rushed to join the Alliance, created local cooperatives for selling crops and purchasing supplies, and petitioned political leaders to create institutions such as government-operated subtreasuries for storing crops and postal banks for extending credit. By 1890, millions of farm families across the country were looking to the Alliance for their salvation.[36]

When Alliance lecturers arrived in North Carolina in 1887, they found Old Bright Belt farm families who were tired of declining prices and high warehouse fees to be a receptive audience to their gospel of rural cooperation.

One organizer described farmers in Wake County, North Carolina—where tobacco was competing with cotton for preeminence—as "ripe fruit" that could be gathered "by a gentle shake of the bush." Taking advantage of the spadework done by the Grange, the Knights of Labor, and, just as important, Leonidas L. Polk's North Carolina Farmers' Association (which he founded about the same time Macune took over the Farmers Alliance), lecturers planted sub-alliances across the North Carolina counties of the Old Bright Belt.[37]

By the summer of 1888, nearly every North Carolina Old Bright Belt county was organized. The editor of the Gold Leaf noted "increased interest in the Alliance" in the region around Henderson: "It is growing in strength and membership, representing many of the best men and farmers in the county." A Stokes County, North Carolina, grower reported in late 1889 that "we now number something over 300 members in the county and still we increase. . . . Our Alliance is growing in interest as well as members." By the election of 1890, supporters of Senator Zebulon Vance in Stokes County warned him that delegates to the county's Democratic Party convention were "over three-fourths Alliancemen," who potentially offered "big opposition" to Vance because of his unwillingness to back the Alliance's program of reform wholeheartedly. The editor of The Greensboro Patriot was disdainful of their complaints, telling Vance he had "raised a row with a lot of sorehead Alliance men."[38]

The Alliance's lecturers also successfully bent the ears of Old Bright Belt growers in Virginia. At its peak, the Alliance claimed roughly 35,000 members across the state; its deepest wells of support were in the state's Old Bright Belt counties. By 1890, every Old Bright county in Virginia from Pittsylvania eastward had a county-level sub-alliance.[39] The Alliance attempted to reach across all lines of tenure when appealing to farm families. Historians of the movement in the Old Bright Belt suggest that landowning farmers were most likely to answer the lecturers' call, but some tenants joined as well.[40]

The Alliance did not admit black farmers, but rapid expansion of the Colored Farmers' Alliance into the Old Bright Belt at around the same time gave black farmers their own vehicle for organizing. It also provided a second source of protest. Best understood as the product of a parallel organizing impulse rather than as an adjunct to the Southern Farmers' Alliance, the Colored Farmers' Alliance originated in Texas in 1886 and quickly built networks of members across the South.[41]

Colored Farmers' Alliance organizers worked more quietly than Southern

Farmers' Alliance lecturers lest they face reprisals from angry landlords or creditors, but they made great headway in the Old Bright Belt. It is impossible to quantify much about the membership of the Colored Farmers Alliance because of its secrecy, but leaders claimed a membership of 20,000 across forty-two of Virginia's ninety-five counties in 1891. These farmers, many likely landowners, had many of the same complaints as white farmers of similar status, but perhaps they felt the pressures of low prices and discrimination at the warehouses more acutely.[42]

Some of the Colored Farmers' Alliance's best lecturers called the Old Bright Belt home, which helped the organization immensely. While Walter A. Pattillo of Granville County was not a farmer himself, he used social networks he had developed as a Baptist minister and Republican political operative to build the organization not only at home but across the state. He also published the *Alliance Advocate* from Oxford to publicize the message of the Colored Farmers' Alliance. Across the state line, Frank B. Ivy in Mecklenburg County and Harry C. Green in Brunswick County worked alongside Edward Austin Jr. of Appomattox County and D. C. Beasley of Dinwiddie County (both of which bordered the Old Bright Belt) to organize black farmers. All were presumably men of stature in their communities: for example, Green owned 107 acres, and Ivy was an alumnus of Hampton Institute. In addition, the *Midland Express*, which was published in Mecklenburg County, became the official organ of the Colored Farmers' Alliance in Virginia.[43]

White farmers and black farmers shared many concerns, but the Farmers' Alliance and the Colored Farmers' Alliance approached each other cautiously. White leaders may have understood the importance of organizing with black farmers, but a combination of racism, a reluctance to alienate their own members, and fear of being accused of biracialism by opponents kept them from reaching out with open arms. Black leaders and farmers were also cautious, concerned that too much openness might lead to accusations in their community that the organization had been co-opted and was therefore unreliable. When Elias Carr, head of the North Carolina Farmers' Alliance, offered Walter Pattillo, a black organizer for the Colored Farmers' Alliance, ten dollars to support his work based on the recommendation from a white organizer for the Colored Farmers' Alliance that Pattillo was "perfectly reliable," he revealed both the parsimony and hesitancy with which white Alliance men approached black farmers. When Pattillo agreed to take the money quietly, he did so with a reluctance to deal with white folks that was common among black Alliance members and black farmers in general.[44]

Both the white and black Alliances opened their doors to women, acknowledging the importance of women to the farm economy. It is difficult to ascertain how many women joined, but one historian has estimated that women accounted for one-third to one-half of Alliance members in some parts of North Carolina. One Davidson County sub-alliance had nine men and twenty-two women remaining on its rolls after a purge of those who were delinquent in paying their dues.[45]

White and black farmers, both male and female, likely found the language of labor the Alliances used compelling. While lecturers and leaders spoke often in broad terms of political economy, of trusts and currency, they hit home in their descriptions of how farmers were denied the fruits of their own labor. One Farmers' Alliance supporter framed his complaint in terms of the fact that farmers did work, while warehousemen and buyers did not. Farmers suffered through "elements and insects" and "weeks of broken rest"; warehousemen and buyers just took the "enormous profits" produced by the farmers' labors.[46]

The most fundamental problem of farmers, he argued, was the arrangement of the tobacco auction. There these middlemen were an "organization" working in concert, he claimed, to take farmers' hard-earned money. "When [the farmer] has laid his much sought for 'yellow leaf' in well arranged order at the feet of the organization, he has to step aside, while the mock competition begins, and there with his hands in his breeches pockets and without a word to say, stands in pitiful, helpless, disorganized isolation, watching the farce as it proceeds between the keen-eyed Jew . . . and the calculating Gentile . . . winking and blinking at the auctioneer when they can catch his swiftly revolving orb; as soon as he receives the mouse's share he is politely bowed out, and kindly told to call again."[47] Railroads, banks, and distant "trusts" did not concern Old Bright Belt farmers as much as the predators they saw at home, the "organization" that exploited their lack of power on the auction floor.[48]

Old Bright Belt Alliance members, white and black, responded well to the Alliances' strategy of cooperation and embraced it as the solution to the problem of the auctions. When attempts to push legislators to take action were unsuccessful, they opened their own warehouses. Unlike the Grange-owned warehouse, which had been limited to Danville, the Alliance opened auction houses across the Old Bright Belt. The first opened in 1888 in Oxford, one of North Carolina's most rapidly growing market towns. A few weeks later, another opened in neighboring Vance County. By 1889, there were Alliance warehouses in Raleigh, High Point, and Danville, and by 1891, the Alliance controlled warehouses in Winston, Henderson, and Clarksville as well.[49]

Because support for the Alliance was rooted almost entirely in growers' anger about the tobacco market, Old Bright Belt growers often disagreed about the value of other programs the larger Alliance movements advocated. One Granville County grower's motion that each sub-alliance appoint a "rotten egg committee" to shower eggs on any speaker who flattered farmers as "the backbone of the country" suggests that at least some had little patience for pablum. County alliances passed resolutions and individual Alliance men wrote letters in support of the free coinage of silver, regulation of the railroads, and the subtreasury plan, by which government-owned warehouses would store crops until they could be sold at better prices and provide loans to farmers, but other members sometimes balked. "I am Alliance all thro 16 oz. to the pound," one supporter wrote, "but I am down on . . . the Sub-treasury humbug." Another member concurred: "Many of we Alliance men do not like the 'Sub Treasury' plan."[50]

Even some leaders were not enamored with the Alliance's one-size-fits-all approach. In 1890, the secretary of the Granville County Farmers' Alliance Tobacco Manufacturing Company argued that the subtreasury system was ill suited to tobacco and that the Alliance should open its own warehouses instead to "make an advance" on members' leaves and "hold them until the trust will pay value for them." The individual farmer, he reasoned, "must sell [and] cannot hold it himself, but if the tobacco was stored . . . money can be drawn on it" in sufficient amounts to allow the "farmer to wait." In 1892, the Border Alliance, which met in Danville and was purported to be "largest and most influential alliance" in both Virginia and North Carolina, debated a motion to separate from the national organization to pursue its own goals. "The interest of the farmers in the tobacco belt are not identical with the interests of farmers elsewhere," supporters of the motion claimed. They lost. The motion may have represented infiltration by anti-Alliance men—tensions between the Alliance and warehousemen had grown heated by this time—but it likely that some of the Alliance growers believed their localized problems with the market were more pressing and more easily solved than the nation's farm problem writ large.[51]

Whatever the power of this dissent in the white and black Alliances, other concerns soon swamped the organization. As the farm question became more politicized after 1892, both white and black farmers left their Alliances.

Some moved to the Peoples' Party (the Populists), giving the insurgent third party a number of important victories, especially in North Carolina. Most, however, retreated to their respective political parties. White farmers feared that any sort of fusion with black voters might tar them as proponents of racial mixing, while black farmers dared not weaken what institutional strength remained in the Republican Party. Talk of fixing the ills of the tobacco market died down, the Alliance warehouses closed their doors, and the sub-alliances that remained focused on cooperative buying for the members who remained.[52]

Old Bright Belt farmers continued to protest market conditions even after the failure of the Alliances, but the target shifted from the warehouses to the American Tobacco Company, which, tightened its hold on the market in the 1890s. As James B. Duke bought out rival tobacco companies, the number of factory buyers dwindled. At the same time, the company wielded its considerable economic power to reduce the ability of independent leaf dealers and speculators to profit. In 1890, for example, the ATC rushed to purchase all leaves known as "cutters" to prevent speculators from having access to them. For the next decade, the company refused to buy from speculators at all and drove many out of business.

Farmers initially welcomed this check on speculation, but they soon realized that the ATC was to blame for low prices. "When much tobacco was bought for speculation, the bidding and buying were spirited and lively," one farmer claimed in 1900, perhaps nostalgically. "No man could tell or guess how much a pile of tobacco would bring. Then the auctioneering was pertinent and helpful to farmers. But now, since the great bulk of the weed is bought by the American Tobacco Company, which fixes the prices to be paid for the several grades to buyers in the various tobacco towns, all genuine competition has ceased." By the early twentieth century, the ATC was buying up nearly half of the tobacco crop in North Carolina alone, giving it great influence over the price it would pay and, by extension, the price its dwindling competition would pay as well. "Time and time again," one supporter of the farmers claimed in 1906, he had heard warehousemen tell disappointed farmers, "I know it, John, I got you the limit." "What's the limit?" he asked. "Why the price set by the heads of the tobacco trust in New York City."[53]

Low prices spurred farmers to organize. Organizers set out across the Old Bright Belt to rally growers. Like the Alliance's lecturers, organizers of these early-twentieth-century protest organizations tapped into farmers' perceptions that their quality of life was declining in relation to that of urban people.

"It is often flippantly asserted that the key to agricultural prosperity is in the diversification of crops, and the raising of home supplies," declared organizer J. Bryan Grimes. "This is true . . . but even then there must a margin of profit to educate his family and secure for them some of the comforts of life, and when agriculture ceases to be sufficiently remunerative for this there is something radically wrong with the economic conditions prevailing." Organizers suggested that farmers limit their acreage and pool their crops in order to compel the ATC (and, by extension, other buyers) to pay higher prices.[54]

Unlike the Alliance, the early-twentieth-century organization identified specifically with the problems and aims of tobacco farmers, as its ever-evolving names suggest. It began as the Tobacco Growers' Protective Association, which became the Inter-State Tobacco Growers' Association, which ultimately became the Mutual Protective Association of the Bright Tobacco Growers of Virginia and North Carolina. Members of the group assumed that their tobacco was a unique product—hence the use of the term "bright tobacco" in the final iteration of the organization's name—and they believed that if they got all farmers to agree to cooperate, they could restrict the quantities that were available and thus force prices higher. Annual meetings in Danville, Durham, South Boston, Virginia, and other Old Bright Belt towns attracted a few hundred attendees. "There were at least 500 people in the church, including the ladies," a reporter noted of a 1907 meeting in Pilot Mountain, North Carolina. In 1906, a reported 1,000 growers pledged that they would turn over at least half of their crops to the Mutual Protective Association of Bright Tobacco Growers of Virginia and North Carolina for storage and resale at a later date.[55]

Getting farm families to actually hold their crops proved difficult. Despite organizer J. F. Jordan's claim that "growers all over the bright tobacco [region] . . . have expressed their intention of holding their tobacco," the organizations had no way to enforce compliance with pledges to reduce crops or deliver them to the cooperatives. Sales figures from Danville suggest that the number of actual cooperators was quite small.[56]

Old Bright Belt growers seemed to like the theory of pooling but showed little interest in supporting it with more than words. For some, structural problems prevented them. Tenants, sharecroppers, and small landowners with crop liens had little ability to participate in pooling because of the need to deliver their crops or repay their loans by the end of the year. Pooling the entire crop or even receiving a partial payment in anticipation of selling it later were simply not options for these farmers. Even relatively independent landowners, however, proved reluctant to cut their acreages or turn over their crops at venues other than the auctions. Where was the incentive to reduce acreage if one's neighbors refused to do the same and a large crop pushed prices downward? Similarly, why not take advantage of the higher prices produced by a short crop and keep a large acreage in tobacco? None of the organizations had enforcement mechanisms, and moral suasion could only go so far.

Unlike in the Tennessee and Kentucky "Black Patch," where arson and other violence became tools for enforcing cooperation with the Planters' Protective Association of that region, only limited violence accompanied the creation of the cooperatives in the Old Bright Belt. No doubt concerned that reports out of the Black Patch would undercut their message, the Bright Belt cooperatives eschewed violence. Nevertheless, in 1908, a few prominent planters in Pittsylvania and Caswell Counties reported that night riders had threatened to tear up their fields or burn their barns, and one "prominent" Davidson County farmer reported that his beds had been destroyed by night. The reports created tension, but rumors swelled that the cooperative's opponents had posted them to discredit supporters of pooling. Some even said the signs were the product of a cruel jokester.[57]

The challenge for organizers of cooperatives lay in trying to convince enough growers to give up the auction system. It was a difficult job for a number of reasons. Some large growers held stakes in warehouses. Others held that it was simply the distortion of the market by the American Tobacco Company, not the auction system itself that was the problem. Still others looked at the auction as a bet they might win with enough hard work. Some believed elites when they said that uprooting the auction system would bankrupt them all. The editor of *Southern Planter* warned farmers not to "antagonize" the region's sources of capital and thus "kill the goose that has laid the golden eggs of the past." The president of the Danville Tobacco Association similarly cautioned those seeking to reduce the crop that attempts to "force prices" upward would "necessitate or invite the use of substitutes for our product. . . . It . . . behooves us . . . to raise sufficiently large crops to supply the domestic and foreign demand at fair profits," he told growers, "rather than small crops at fictitious prices" that would lead buyers "to grow tobacco like ours in foreign countries with labor at three cents to ten cents per diem wages."[58]

To counter resistance, organizers tried to convince farmers that cooperation was the only way to defend their status. "The farmers need to organize

for self-preservation," T. B. Parker, the secretary of the North Carolina Tobacco Growers' Association urged members around 1900. Speaking largely
to white male farmers, he presented the problems of Old Bright Belt growers,
especially the problem of the ATC, as threats to their position that demanded
community effort. "By organization," he told them, "the Tobacco Growers
can maintain their position, their respect, their manhood. Without it . . . they
will have lost much that our forefathers held dear—independence."[59]

The arrival of the National Farmers' Union in the Old Bright Belt raised
the volume on this kind of language. Formed in Texas in 1902 by leaders
who, in the words of historian Theodore Saloutos, "believed that the farmer
was a selfish individual who was disposed to cooperate more readily with a
producer of the same commodity," the National Farmers' Union seemed to
offer the perfect organizational vehicle for Old Bright Belt farmers hoping
to convince their neighbors it was in their best economic interest to chan-
nel their economic self-interest through a cooperative. Organizers came to
North Carolina in 1905 and entered Virginia shortly thereafter. They found
some of their strongest support in the Old Bright Belt. By 1912, every North
Carolina Old Bright Belt county was organized, with the strongest support in
the western counties where small white farmers dominated. Congressional
hearings in 1914 indicated that Virginia's Old Bright Belt counties were well
represented among the state leaders of the Farmers' Union.[60]

Echoing the strategies of local cooperatives and building on its own model
of cooperative marketing, the Farmers' Union encouraged farmers to pool
their crops. In 1911, farm families across the Old Bright Belt began to pool
their crops; in Stokes County, a reported 90 percent of growers agreed to the
plan. According to the agreement, growers would receive a percentage of the
value of the crop at the time of delivery with the promise of receiving the
remainder of the money after the Farmers' Union sold the crops. They even
established a dry prizery like those operated by American Tobacco Company
in order to dry the leaves and store them indefinitely for later sale.[61]

The Farmers' Union continued to pool for the next several years, but the
plan was mostly unsuccessful. Rumors of mismanagement followed and
farmers complained that they never received the full value of their crops.
"Prices did go up," one bemused grower recalled two decades later, "but I
never collected the full amount due me." Bitterness increased, and members
left the Farmers' Union in droves.[62]

The failure of the Farmers' Union was not just about business, though.
Like the earlier cooperatives, it failed to tap into the changing nature of

tobacco farming in the Old Bright Belt. It sought only white farmers as members—the Virginia division's founding document expressly forbade the admission of "negroes or persons of African descent"—ignoring the growing number of black landowners in the Old Bright Belt, who with other black farmers in the region constituted a sizable constituency. Organizers also tended to echo the condescension of elites toward tenants and sometimes disparaged sharecroppers and others who relied on family labor. A 1914 resolution by the tobacco-growing members of the Virginia Farmers' Union described tenants as destructive to both the tobacco crops and the land. These tenants, one member explained, reduced the wage labor force. Instead of working for others and forcing their children to do the same, he claimed, tenants "keep their children at home and get a small wage for themselves and their children." Such attitudes doubtless hurt the Farmers' Union's chances of bringing more tobacco farmers into the fold.[63]

By World War I, the Farmers' Union was largely moribund and paralyzed by its inability to build coalitions and convince farm families that it could secure them the prosperity and dignity they desired. Farm families, for their part, had largely resigned themselves to the cycle of low prices, content to keep gambling that next year's crop would break the cycle. The Great War convinced many that their waiting had not been in vain.

4

Cooperation

The Great War brought boom times to farming families across the Tobacco South. Driven by the wartime demand for cigarettes for soldiers, tobacco prices skyrocketed to previously unseen highs, and farm families who relied on bright tobacco for their incomes celebrated their newfound prosperity. "Farmers can be seen hugging each other over the amazing prices they are getting, and pinch themselves quite frequently to see if they have been dreaming," one observer reported from the markets in 1917. Having finally seen tobacco pay off, farm families, black and white, rushed to buy consumer goods they had long been denied; they purchased everything from automobiles to indoor plumbing. Many also bought land. "The farmers . . . have made good in growing tobacco," the black Extension Service agent from Mecklenburg County reported in 1917. "It has sold extremely well and many have paid some of their debts which have been standing for years." One extension agent reported that he found it "very hard to talk cooperative warehouses to these farmers" because they were doing so well.[1]

The good years did not last long. In 1920, farm families planted record amounts of tobacco just as wartime demand evaporated and prices plummeted. Discontent followed the opening of the markets. "Tobacco prices have declined from $5.00 to $10.00 on the [Oxford] market during the week," creating "some local agitation" for the markets to be closed, one official reported. In Virginia, farm families were "very much wrought up over the low price of tobacco." While prices were higher than they had been before the war, they were much lower than farmers had anticipated and only got worse as the marketing season wore on.[2]

The shock of low prices renewed calls for cooperation. Leading growers arranged meetings in numerous market towns throughout the fall to discuss the problem; in December, representatives from the states where bright to-bacco was grown met in Richmond to form the Tobacco Growers' Cooperative Association, which became better known as the Tri-State because it organized growers in Virginia, North Carolina, and South Carolina. Farmers sometimes just called it the "Co-ops." Like the Farmers' Union, organizers of the Tri-State hoped to pool members' tobacco and resell later at better prices. Advised by cooperation guru Aaron Sapiro, who had helped organize the Sun-Maid raisin cooperative in California, organizers hoped eventually to control enough production to set their own prices. The Tri-State never did; by 1926, it was in receivership, leaving thousands of farmers embittered.[3]

The Tri-State nevertheless marked a turn in farmers' challenge to the auction system. Probably more than any organizers that came before them, the Tri-State's leaders understood the nature of tobacco farm work by the 1920s and pushed their message not only to black and white men, including land-owners and tenants, but to their families as well. Its leaders' demand that the cooperative focus on tobacco alone echoed farm families' demands, while the scale organizers proposed sought to correct the localism that had long hampered farmers' efforts. Its use of federal resources such as the Extension Service and its reliance on new law that enabled farmers to create their own "trusts" pointed to the future, too, establishing a pattern of farmer-state cooperation that would continue long after the Tri-State's demise.[4]

The Tri-State's charter required that 50 percent of the growers agree to market their tobacco through their warehouses for it to be binding, and orga-nizers began canvassing growers immediately. By 1921, 64,000 farmers from Virginia and the Carolinas had agreed to market their tobacco through the Tri-State. In addition, organizers recruited the support of a number of busi-ness and political leaders, including *Raleigh News and Observer* editor Jose-phus Daniels and Virginia senator Claude Swanson, who signed up his own tobacco crop in 1921. Support was especially strong in the Old Bright Belt.[5]

The Tri-State had a relatively strong, centralized bureaucracy, but build-ing support among average tobacco farmers required hard work on the lo-cal level. Leaders traveled the Old Bright Belt organizing meetings, arrang-ing speakers, and passing out literature. To gain support, organizers turned largely to traditional methods of publicity, including enrollment campaigns that resembled religious revivals or political rallies. "They had big all-day meetings with picnic dinners and barbeque suppers and brunswick [*sic*] stews all over that neighborhood," a witness to one of the campaigns re-membered. "We used to go to all of them and listen to the speeches. I don't remember what that man's name was that came to our neighborhood, but he was a natural-born orator. The farmers just stood there with their mouths open to listen to him. It sounded like a good revival sermon before he got through and it went home the same way."[6]

The Tri-State also benefited from work of Extension Service county agents. Created by the 1914 Smith-Lever Act, the Extension Service employed county agents to educate farmers about the latest agricultural innovations. The Extension Service also employed home demonstration agents, who encouraged farm women to purchase modern household conveniences and aspire to an urban middle-class standard of living. By 1920, both male and female agents had begun to make inroads in communities throughout the Old Bright Belt. Defining their work broadly, the Extension Service directors of Virginia and the Carolinas dispatched county and home demonstration agents to sign up farmers for the Tri-State; the directors saw this as an opportunity to help farmers while expanding the influence of the Extension Service. The work generally followed the gendered division of labor constituted in the organization of the Extension Service; county agents largely worked to sign up male farmers while home demonstration agents approached women for support. These agents worked long hours to convince farmers and their families of the benefits of selling their tobacco cooperatively, and their labor clearly helped the fledgling organization get off the ground. "I . . . put my shoulder to the wheel," one agent boasted in 1922, "and went to work with the farmer, doing what he asked, going where he requested, driving night and day, getting up meetings, making talks, familiarizing myself with cooperative marketing; and preaching cooperation, organization and loyalty."[7]

Clarence Poe, the region's leading agricultural journalist, also lent his talents to the Tri-State's cause. As editor of *The Progressive Farmer*, Poe had been trying for years to convince farm families to organize and he saw the Tri-State as their salvation. While Poe's editorial page preached to those outside the Tri-State, the cooperative's leaders shepherded the flock through the pages of the *Tri-State Tobacco Grower*. Both used producerist rhetoric that appealed to farm families' sense of the value of their own work, albeit often in ways that resonated best with white male farmers. "Surely our sturdy Anglo-Saxon Southern white farmers are not going to be content with industrial slavery . . . [or] to acknowledge somebody else as 'master' in fixing a price on the product of [their] own labor," Poe implored in 1921. "Every real Big Man in the United States is in favor of cooperative marketing," the *Tri-State*

Tobacco Grower trumpeted the following year, "Only 'pinhookers' and men who make money out of the 'auction' system are against it."[8]

Despite the use of race-based language by prominent supporters, the Tri-State broke the pattern of segregation that marked the Farmers' Union and reached out to black and white tobacco farmers alike. Black farm families were central to the bright tobacco economy, especially in eastern North Carolina and South Carolina, where sharecropping was more prevalent, and organizers understood that excluding African Americans would simply be counterproductive. Black Extension Service agents led much of this work and held meetings for black farmers across the region. The Tri-State's organizers also reached out to black farmers through the journal published at Hampton Institute, *The Southern Workman*. "The small tobacco grower who is now exploited—whether he be black or white—will be protected under the co-operative plan," Virginia Tri-State secretary Sydney D. Frissell wrote. He openly acknowledged the talents and hopes of black farmers. "Sixty percent of our tobacco growers—white and black—are burdened with crop mortgages, he wrote, expressing an astonishing level of solidarity. "But victory in their drive for economic independence means that our farmers stand to gain that independence which they dreamed they had, the hours which their children lost from school while hoeing in the fields, the kind of homes of which their wives have dreamed, and comforts which their toil has fairly earned." He concluded, "Here is inter-racial cooperation earnest and unquestioning, effectively at work to bring about a better day for white and black alike."[9]

Efforts to recruit black farmers proved successful. "Both White and Negro Farmers in this County are successfully demonstrating that Tobacco can be marketed cooperatively," one Extension Service agent reported in 1922. The cooperative's openness to black farmers had its limits, though: most met in segregated locals and no black members rose to any sort of leadership in the organization. Nevertheless, its openness sets the Tri-State cooperative apart as one of the few biracial rural reform organizations between the demise of the Populists in the 1890s and the rise of groups such as the Southern Tenant Farmers' Union in the 1930s.[10]

The leadership of the Tri-State was most effective in convincing families who owned small to medium-sized farms to join. The 1920 price crash affected these farmers as much or more than any other group, in part because the low prices threatened to erode the gains they had made during the war years. The Tri-State had less success convincing large landowners to join. Landlords, in fact, regularly barred their renters and sharecroppers from joining the Tri-State despite court judgments defending their right to sell their shares however they pleased. Virginian E. A. Jackson reported that his landlord told him not "to deliver any . . . tobacco to the 'Co-ops' until he was paid." Jackson ignored his landlord's order and sold to the Tri-State, but others had little choice but to deliver their crops as their landlords or other creditors directed.[11]

To strengthen the organization, Tri-State organizers worked especially hard to build fervor among entire farm families, especially farm women. They hired one woman to edit a special page dedicated to women's activities in the *Tri-State Tobacco Grower* and another to travel the back roads to organize farm women. In their efforts, they pointed to the blurry line that separated household economies from the tobacco auction market. "When the farmer fails to get a decent price for his products," Poe wrote, "he takes it out of his standards of living. He must do so. He has to get along without the improvements he and his wife desire in the way of a better home, lights, paint, waterworks, together with better school advantages for the children." Organizers used language rooted in the rural progressivism that was popular in the early twentieth century and portrayed women's involvement as critical to solving the problems facing tobacco farm families. "Tobacco growers have had few chances in the last fifty years to sell at a profit and in fifty years a million boys have left the farms of Virginia and the Carolinas. We have the system, but not the boys to blame," one editor wrote in 1922. "With cooperative marketing . . . country life [will] become worth living."[12]

The appeals touched a nerve. Mrs. Ed Carraway wrote to explain that despite the fact that she and her husband owned their land, lived economically, and "worked in the crop rain or shine, early and late," they had "no fund to carry our children to a higher education." The market schedule, she argued, put farmers at a disadvantage and even threatened the morality of family members. "Farmers not having the money . . . were forced to eat in cheap places and camp in the camp rooms of a warehouse with hundreds of other men. Now . . . do you think your boy could go to these crowded markets . . . and come back home the boy he was before he left?" The Tri-State, she continued, was the only solution to the problem, as it would make the selling process less time consuming: "As I understand it, a load of tobacco will be unloaded, graded, a bill of sale given with check and receipted at once, and thereby save time." Time saved and idle hands kept from the devil: a farm mother's dream come true.[13]

Since the Tri-State counted only heads of households as members, it is impossible to quantify how many women responded as Mrs. Carraway did, but it is clear that many women did work to support the Tri-State. Women organized meetings; served as secretaries; wrote letters, poems, and songs about the cooperative; and did hundreds of other tasks to build the membership and keep it faithful. "One of the best locals we have has a woman for secretary," the editor of the *Tri-State Tobacco Grower* reported in 1924. "She helps the chairman plan an interesting program for every meeting and members of this local do not break their contracts because they know what it is all about and have their eyes fixed on the goal." Maude Barnard Browne submitted a meeting program to the *Tri-State Tobacco Grower* that included time for community singing, a Bible lesson, and several poetry readings in addition to discussion of regular business. The meeting's theme, "Love of Fellow-men," aimed to remind flagging members of their obligation to honor their contracts. A Warren County, North Carolina, farm woman echoed this sentiment in a song entitled "Come to the Co-op Meeting." Set to the tune of the traditional hymn "There's a Church in the Wildwood," the song encouraged farmers to remain loyal to the Tri-State by hearkening to the promise of cooperation: "If the farmers would all pull together / There would be no more mortgage on the mule; / They would be as rich as city people / And could send their girls and boys off to school."[14]

Despite the Tri-State's recognition of women's importance to the organization and the willingness of its leaders to include women in its leadership, supporters of women's involvement in the cooperative's activities retained sexist cultural assumptions about the proper channels for women's work. Although women's field labor helped see the crop from seedbed to market, their domestic work mitigated the burden of low tobacco prices, and many actually controlled some portion of the crop, leaders of cooperatives saw farm women as secondary, supportive actors in the production of bright tobacco.

The Tri-State's policy regarding the tobacco grown by the wives and children of members also reflected organizers' assumptions about women's and children's work. Organizers argued that a farm woman or child who controlled a portion of a crop that was signed over to the cooperative was obligated to sell her share at the cooperative with the rest of the crop. "There is no reason why the tobacco sold by the wives and children of our members should be sold other than through the Tobacco Growers Cooperative Association," the editor of the *Tri-State Tobacco Grower* explained, "and each member will be expected and required to deliver the tobacco grown by his wife and children to the point which he has chosen as his delivery point."[15] When farm women complained about the policy, Tri-State leaders printed letters like the one from Virginian Lillie Smith, who gushed about the first payment she received from the Tri-State after her husband took her crop to be sold cooperatively over her protests. The publication of such letters was an attempt to diffuse women's anger by reminding them of the greater purpose of cooperation. "I am [a] colored woman," Smith explained, "and hope that every colored woman and man will join the association at once if they market tobacco, for we have fed Mr. Warehouseman for a long time, and his auction gang."[16]

Not all farm women rushed to help the Tri-State. Amy Harris chafed at the requirement that she deliver her portion of the crop to the Tri-State because her father was a member. "I think being I am 21 years old I ought to have the right to sell my tobacco," she explained. Her letter received the customary response that selling through the cooperative would benefit her more in the long run. Other farm women actively undermined the Tri-State by helping their husbands sell their tobacco fraudulently on the open market when they grew frustrated with the cooperative. "There are women, too numerous to mention," one Virginia farm woman complained in 1925, "who are claiming that they own the team and everything (or allowing the men to say they do, which amounts to the same thing) in order to put the tobacco on the auction floor, and there are others who 'claim' to be hiring men of the family to make tobacco for them."[17]

These women did not bring down the Tri-State. A broader lack of support did that. Most tobacco farm families never joined the Tri-State, and many who signed the contract did not remain faithful to it. In 1925, the Danville Tobacco Association estimated that the Tri-State handled only about 16.5 percent of the crop, a far cry from the monopoly organizers had hoped to build across the bright tobacco belt. In earlier years support had been greater, but frustration with a payout system that never paid farmers all the money due them, concerted campaigns by warehouse owners to discredit the Tri-State's leaders, rumors of poor accounting and corruption, and the outright intimidation of some members by warehousemen and landlords all contributed to an erosion of support for the organization over time.[18]

Prices fell again once the Tri-State failed. "The . . . tobacco farmer is just as badly discouraged to day as they [sic] were in 1920 or any other year in the past," one North Carolina grower claimed in 1928. And things only got worse. Prices fell further in 1929 and continued to slide through the 1932 season, when they reached prewar lows. Many farmers sold their crops "below the cost of production," one Extension Service agent reported, "leaving the average farmer in a rather poverty stricken condition." The depressed conditions placed increasing pressure on growers of all classes. Sharecropping increase, and according to one observer, "quite a few" landowners "sold out and left the country." Young men left home in search of "something better than farming" instead of entering the ranks of sharecroppers as so many of their fathers had done.[19]

The flight of sons and daughters from the land placed a great strain on farm families. While many maintained ties with family members on the farm, returning on weekends and during busy seasons to help, their exodus destabilized the farm labor situation in the region. "Most of our young men have gone to [the] cities," one Virginia farmer complained. The pressure to take public work, another observer explained, "causes unrest and dissatisfaction" with farm work, leading more to "quit the farm . . . and labor in factories." The "steady cash income" of the region's factories, he later noted, caused the "farming population to drift" from the farms which, in turn, "unbalance[d] the situation." Many farm families, in other words, were coming undone.[20]

The pressures on families spurred further calls for organization. The Tri-State experience soured many on the idea of agricultural cooperation, but when organizers hoping to create a new cooperative under the aegis of the newly created Federal Farm Board put out the call to come to Danville in February 1930, over 2,000 Virginia and North Carolina farmers responded. Many were from the Old Bright Belt. Support soon wavered, however, and the organization could not get enough commitment from growers to go forward.[21]

Farm families seemed to agree that reducing production and marketing crops cooperatively were the keys to raising tobacco prices, but no one wanted to sign up their crops unless their neighbors could be compelled to do the same. In 1931, North Carolina growers pressed the state to impose mandatory tobacco controls, a move Virginia growers applauded. "A number of tobacco growers in this section have expressed themselves in favor of this or any other method that would curtail the size of the tobacco crop," reported the *South Hill Enterprise*. At a meeting in Boydton, Virginia, growers went so far as to call for a 50 percent reduction in tobacco acreage, provided growers in the Carolinas and Georgia agreed to do the same. That same year, growers in Stokes County, North Carolina, pledged to cut 20 percent of their crops. However, none of these pledges were enforceable, and they were all doomed to failure.[22]

Franklin Roosevelt's New Deal soon offered the means for enforcing controls. Reducing the volume of agricultural production was among the first goal of New Dealers, and the low prices of 1932—when tobacco garnered about as much as it had in 1914—convinced them that tobacco had to be on the list of commodities covered by the sweeping Agricultural Adjustment Act of 1933. Passed in the heady urgency of Franklin Roosevelt's first 100 days, the AAA expanded the state's reach into the countryside as never before by establishing the legislative groundwork for crop controls for the nation's chief commodities, including cotton, rice, corn, and wheat. Tobacco was the only crop on the list that was neither a food nor fiber, but New Dealers felt that it should be included because of its critical role in the rural economy of so many places, especially in the South.

The resulting Federal Tobacco Program, while complex in its particulars, was generally straightforward in purpose. A series of laws, beginning with the 1933 Agricultural Adjustment Act, then the 1934 Kerr-Smith Tobacco Act, and finally the 1938 Agricultural Adjustment Act, created its legal framework. Together, the laws aimed to bring national production in line with projected consumption by first establishing acreage limits—"allotments"—for each tobacco farm and then using a carrot-and-stick approach to force farm families to abide by them. Farmers who remained within their allotted acreages received guaranteed minimum prices designed to keep their incomes in line with those of urban workers. Farmers whose acreage exceeded their allotments paid a 50 percent tax on the money their crops made at auction. The Federal Tobacco Program wedded two forces growers had long tried to harness: democracy and power. By requiring that two-thirds of growers approve for its provisions to be binding, the program gave growers a voice in choosing whether to be regulated, while its sharp penalties provided solid defenses against those who would cheat it. The program enjoyed widespread support across the Tobacco South, but especially in the Old Bright Belt, where approval of the program usually exceeded 90 percent.[23]

Old Bright Belt families had good reason to support the program. Besides price supports, the allotment system froze the geography and scale of tobacco agriculture. Before the 1930s, the Old Bright Belt had faced increasing competition from growers further south who were giving up cotton as competition from western cotton growers increased. Had the progress of bright tobacco agriculture not been halted by the allotment program, the bulk of bright tobacco production likely would have expanded further south. Old Bright Belt growers, with their small acreages, would have been harder pressed in their competition with large growers and in all likelihood would have had to turn to other crops.

The design was not accidental. John B. Hutson and J. Con Lanier, two of the Federal Tobacco Program's architects, were among the closest things to organic intellectuals in the U.S. Department of Agriculture (USDA). Hutson, the son of Kentucky tobacco farmers, had made a career out of knowing the ins and outs of the global tobacco trade while working for the Department of Agricultural Economics. Appointed to head the Tobacco Division of the new Agricultural Adjustment Administration, Hutson selected Lanier, a lawyer, landowner, warehouseman, and former mayor of Greenville, North Carolina (a major New Bright Belt auction town), as his assistant. Hutson and Lanier designed strict production enforcement provisions that were unique among the New Deal's adjustment programs. They reflected the demands of growers who argued that steep penalties for failing to participate in the program were the only way to keep farmers behind it. "The farmers of this county feel," one observer explained, "that . . . tobacco farmers of the South should be protected from those who would chisel in and counteract the effects of the signers by planting a large acreage as the few who have not signed the contract and those who have not been raising tobacco are intending to do." Or, as another put it, "I find overwhelming sentiment in favor of some legislation which will put all tobacco growers on an even basis."[24]

The addition of standardized grading to the program in the late 1930s helped farm families counter another challenge of the auction: the control tobacco manufacturers had to define the quality of leaves. Federal grading actually antedated the New Deal. In 1925, at the behest of the Tri-State, the USDA attempted to use provisions of the 1916 Warehouse Act to establish standard grades for tobacco. The first federal graders went to work in 1929 on the auction floors in one market town in each tobacco belt. At first federal grading was voluntary and nonbinding, and growers had to pay to have their crops graded. For this reason, relatively few used the service. At South Hill, Virginia, the Old Bright Belt's only market with government grading that first year, only 19 percent of growers had their crops graded, but it piqued the interest of plenty of others. The *South Hill Enterprise* reported that "many farmers from a distance have visited the market and conferred with the government graders in reference to the grading work."[25] The following year, the arrival of two graders on the auction floors of Henderson, North Carolina, generated interest from growers. "Use of this service is steadily growing in favor," the local extension agent reported, adding that they were grading "twenty to twenty[-]five thousand pounds per week" by the end of the season. Orange County, North Carolina, growers traveled to Smithfield (in North Carolina's New Bright Belt) to see the graders at work, but when they petitioned their local board of trade to apply for graders, they were rebuffed.[26]

It is hardly surprising that the warehousemen on the board of trade rejected the proposal. They resented any incursions on their traditional domain and argued that graders could add nothing but another level of bureaucracy. The *Danville Register* opined that the arrival of federal graders, "fresh from the files of the Department of Agriculture, will add a touch of comedy to the tragedy of low prices which the farmers are finding everywhere."[27] Resistance grew stronger in the 1930s when Virginia congressman John Flanagan proposed a bill to make grading a mandatory part of the New Deal's tobacco program. "We do not believe Government grading makes tobacco companies pay more for tobacco," one warehouseman explained. Buyers by and large said the same thing. One claimed that compulsory grading "would represent a tremendous outlay on the part of the Government and would serve no constructive purpose." Instead of making the market more efficient," he continued, "it would seriously hinder and impede the orderly marketing of tobacco." Some of the fiercest resistance came from one of the designers of the federal tobacco program. J. Con Lanier argued that the program was simply a ploy to undermine the auction system—something he and Hutson had steadfastly refused to do when planning the tobacco program. "The enemies of the auction system of selling tobacco are giving this Bill their hearty support," he boomed in a published flyer sent to members of Congress, adding that the proposal "is not being advocated for the benefit of the tobacco grower; it is merely an attempt to make a political saddle horse out of the tobacco program for politicians to ride."[28]

In fact, growers felt that grading only improved both the Federal Tobacco Program and the auction system. Members of the Granville County Pomona Grange believed that the service had a "tendency to stabilize . . . prices and to protect farmers who are not familiar with the . . . grades and prevailing prices." Another North Carolina landowner agreed, writing that the system allowed him to send his tenants to market without having to worry that they would not receive the best prices. "I have my crop graded and know that I was well paid by doing so. A glance at the Government Daily Report [and] one can tell what his grade[s] of tobacco are selling for from day to day." Virginia growers who had worked with the graders at South Hill praised the system's ability to thwart pinhookers and shady buyers by allowing grower to sell their tobacco "with out [*sic*] loss through speculation and manipulation." Growers made it clear that they wanted a regulated marketplace, not "the return of the old auction system of tobacco."[29]

With the mechanisms for controlling production and regularizing grading in place, the only thing farm families lacked was a system for cooperative selling. That came next. In the fall of 1939, British buyers stopped buying U.S. tobacco when World War II began. Unwilling to let the disappearance of these important buyers undermine the fragile tobacco program, Federal Tobacco Program administrators worked out a plan for the government to purchase tobacco on the market for later sale to Great Britain. This program continued throughout the war. The USDA's Commodity Credit Corporation (CCC) bought leaf on the auction floors and resold it to Lend-Lease program suppliers for sale abroad.[30]

The collapse of prices immediately after the war spurred administrators to continue the practice of government purchase, but under the direction of a private entity. In the summer of 1946, the Flue-Cured Tobacco Cooperative Stabilization Corporation, usually just called Stabilization, took over management of the program. It was a grower-owned cooperative; all allotment owners were members. Stabilization became the buyer of last resort and purchased whatever tobacco manufacturers did not want. It paid parity prices using CCC loans, then processed, stored, and resold the tobacco to manufacturers to pay off the loans. No tobacco farm family ever had to worry again that the leaves they worked so hard to bring to market would go unsold.

Farmers did not defeat the auction system by building their own warehouses, and they did not bring the tobacco companies to their knees by controlling the market through cooperatives. Instead, they found a partner in the federal government, which had the power to exert control over both themselves and the market in ways that drew on the rough communitarianism that had supported the most successful protests of the previous half-century. The Federal Tobacco Program inscribed the small, family-operated farm as the norm, something farm families had struggled to do for years in the face of planter disparagement. As one Extension Service agent put it, the program allowed farm families to do "something they had always wanted to do for themselves."[31]

5

Stabilization

In 1962, sensing that postwar changes in American agriculture were making farmers uneasy about the future, Stephen E. Wrather, director of the tobacco division of the USDA's Agricultural Marketing Service, sought to ease the minds of the farm families whose loyalty it was his job to cultivate. "Tobacco may be providing a last stronghold for the traditional 'family farm' in the United States," he wrote in 1962. The number of tobacco farms was increasing despite a significant decline in the number of farms nationwide, he told them, and the crop's comparatively high cash returns per acre enabled tobacco farm families to survive, even thrive, as small growers of other crops found themselves squeezed out by their larger neighbors. He heaped special praise on the Federal Tobacco Program, noting that it had prevented the massive surpluses seen in other commodity programs. "Indications are that there will be a continuing decline in the number of small and medium size farms and that fewer and fewer families will earn a living from the land. However, the historical place of tobacco in American agriculture is expected to remain stable."[1]

Newspapers across the country responded to this report. Most presented his findings dispassionately. Some tobacco-state newspapers cheered a bit. Only the conservative *Chicago Tribune*, whose editors had loathed New Deal programs from the outset, challenged his assertions. Offering that his was a "Burocrat's View of the Family Farm," the editor declared that Wrather had "a strange conception of the family farm." "Tobacco is the most highly subsidized and the most stringently controlled crop in the United States," the paper asserted, yet few farmers could "make a living solely by growing tobacco," because "restrictions are so tough . . . that allotments are issued not in terms of halves or quarters of an acre but in hundredths of an acre." The program was "nothing more than government allocation of the right to produce, a notion consistent with socialism but wholly inconsistent with the private enterprise system."[2]

Old Bright Belt farm families likely would have taken umbrage at the editor's assertion that their program was a threat to capitalism. On the contrary, most would have argued, the Federal Tobacco Program was the fulfillment of the nation's long obligation to its farmers. "The tobacco program has been the most successful agricultural program ever inaugurated in the country," boomed Virginia's John Flannagan, the longtime champion of small tobacco farmers, on the floor of Congress in 1945. Most growers agreed heartily.[3]

Their enthusiasm was understandable. The program had largely stabilized tobacco prices, flattening the cyclical peaks and valleys that had characterized the market for decades. At the same time, high levels of price supports pushed tobacco prices higher and supported an improved standard of living for most tobacco farmers, especially landowners. The program's strict restrictions on moving allotments between farms placed a check on the consolidation of acreage that existed among growers of other crops and enabled many small farmers to mitigate the pressure to get big or get out. Farm families understood better than the editor how slashed allotments pinched them, yet the vast majority continued to vote for the program's continuation because they knew what unbridled production for a free market would mean for them. Memories of the low prices that followed the rejection of production controls in 1938—the only year they voted against them—haunted tobacco farm families for more than a generation.

Yet at the same time, Old Bright Belt farm families certainly knew that the world Wrather described was a fantasy. His statistics were misleading, his assertions about supply and demand were strained, and his optimism was misplaced. Thousands of farm families, especially the landless and small landowners, were leaving the land as surplus tobacco sat in storage waiting for buyers who would never come and untold numbers of production allotments went unused. Many farm families were not so sure about their future. At the same time, they confronted increasingly complex regimentation as the Federal Tobacco Program dictated not only how much they could grow but also what they could grow and how they could grow it.

Despite this, they saw in the Federal Tobacco Program the means for confronting modernization on their own terms. In its byzantine regulations they found stability they had never known before. Stability was illusory at best, though, especially for the family labor system farm families cherished.

There is no denying that the Federal Tobacco Program did its job. By the mid-1930s, tobacco prices had rebounded and many farm families were able to make a living from the land again. "The increase in prices which has resulted from the program," one county Extension Service agent noted in 1935, "has meant in many instances the saving of homes from foreclosure, it has meant the return to school of children who had been withdrawn for lack of adequate clothing and books, it has meant in many cases, the lifting of a burden of debt which has caused untold worry, amounting almost to hopelessness." He added hopefully, "The ideal of a self-sufficing farm [has been] more nearly realized than ever before."[4]

Not everyone was as sanguine. It soon became apparent that New Deal policies had unintended consequences for the region's traditional family labor system. Reports of families hard pressed to make do on reduced acreages proliferated. North Carolina grower W. S. McKinney, who blasted the tobacco program as "obnoxious" and "unjust," complained that cutting his son's planned nine-acre crop down to a 3.5-acre allotment unfairly limited his initiative and harmed the sharecropping family on his land. His son, he explained, "has a wife, 3 bright little kids, two big mules that cost him 600 dollars, 2 tobacco barns, a share cropper who has a wife and 3 little kids[,] making ten on his farm. How can he stand it?" Others argued that the allotment system was ill fitted to conditions in the Old Bright Belt and should therefore be adjusted. "90% of eastern [North Carolina] lands are cultivable, while not 30% of upper piedmont is possible tobacco land—and much of that low," one grower complained. "Why handicap the piedmont?" On top of this, rumors that some growers were getting a better deal than others swirled in every neighborhood, stirring up old resentments and class antagonism. "If the adjustment is left up to our Co. Agts. and their co-workers," one grower complained, "it will continue to be ruled by politics and graft. Some will get more favors than justly due them while the little fellow will suffer." Some pushed for protection for the smallest growers. "Justice is *justice*," expounded one grower. "[Reductions] should not apply to the small farmer . . . Every man that already has a barn on his place should be allowed at least 3 acres," since this "is considered about the capacity of a barn."[5]

Allotments especially hurt tenant families. In an effort to maintain their own viability, many landowners cut tenants' acreage first and worked the acreage themselves that they might normally rent out. One Caswell County grower cut his two tenants' acreages in half, from four to two acres, which "result[ed] in a lowered income and much idle labor." While this landowner did what he could to keep both families on his land, others simply stopped renting to tenants. Between 1930 and 1940, the number of sharecropper-worked farms in Old Bright Belt counties decreased by over 15 percent. While this decrease was not as disruptive as it was in other regions—in large part because of the limited extent of sharecropping in the region—it never-theless displaced many families. According to one observer, "tenants moved from one farm to another in order to get a larger acreage of tobacco." When news got out that Eula Jones's Wake County property was available to rent on shares, requests from interested tenants descended on her. "I have dozens and dozens of applications for farms every fall by people who are just beg-ging for a place to live and work," another large landholder reported.[6]

Even for those with access to land, the program brought profound do-mestic dislocations. With less tobacco to grow, families had less need for and less ability to support older children except in the busiest seasons. "It should be said that there are a large number of farmers with unusually small allotments who are indeed hard pressed to make ends meet," the Pittsylvania County Extension Service agent noted in 1935. "In fact there is some doubt as to whether they can continue to operate on such a small allotment, espe-cially in cases where large families are involved." This fueled an increase in the number of people taking off-farm "public" work. In 1935, over a quarter of Virginia's Old Bright Belt farmers (heads of household) reported working off the farm during the previous year. "We have a continued breaking down of farms into almost a 'Henry Ford System,'" an Extension Service agent re-ported from around Winston-Salem; "work in the factory part of the time or some members of the family work in the factories and some on the farm." Margaret Jarman Hagood found that among the white sharecroppers she interviewed, both men and women regularly took on a host of jobs off the farm. "Most common was some source of income . . . earned by the husband from WPA or by working in a filling station on Saturdays, or running a grain mill during the winter, going to Canada to cure tobacco after his own crop was housed, hauling tobacco, driving a meat truck, doing farm work for a neighbor, or hunting or trapping in winter." Taking work off the farm was an option largely for white farmers, but black farmers also found work. Durham County's black Extension Service agent noted that "many of the people only do part time farming" and "depend on their one outstanding crop, tobacco, for partial livelihood."[7]

Public work brought in money, but it had drawbacks. Off-farm work destabilized traditional labor patterns. Time spent in the factory was time not spent in the fields, and in the labor-intensive world of tobacco farming this put more pressure on those at home. In addition, older children who left the farm might never come back, irrevocably altering family relations. Person County grower S. T. Dunn, for example, complained that his small allotment would not be enough to support his children and worried that they would have to take factory work to survive. "I haven't got but 30 acres of land," he explained to Senator Josiah Bailey. "I live near a cotton mill & a weaving mill and I don't want my boys to go to public work[.] I never have & I need them & want to keep them." While we cannot know what Dunn's sons wanted— many young people relished the opportunity to leave the farm behind—it's clear he blamed the tobacco program for aggravating the problem. "All I want is a crop for my boys to encourage them to stay with me. 4,000 lbs. of tobacco at 21 cents is not much inducement for six in a family to make any money."[8]

World War II further disrupted labor arrangements in the Old Bright Belt. The wartime demand for labor accelerated the pace of migration off the farms. Thousands of men and women left for the armed forces, but even more left for work in factories and on military bases. The exodus took workers in their prime off farms, leaving only older people and young children on the land. While they praised their children's service to the war effort, farmers could not but complain about the loss of their best workers. The loss of other traditional sources of hired labor—sharecroppers and local farm laborers— to government or industrial work further compounded the labor shortages. Farmers grumbled that they could not compete with industrial and government wages. "It seems . . . that the farmer is ask[ed] to do more than his share when he [has] to compete with public work that pay[s] so much more for labor," one farmer complained, adding that "lots of farmer[s] are talking about selling their farms and going to defense projects."[9]

To address the shortages, farm families first intensified their use of traditional sources of labor. Women and children became more conspicuous in the fields, as did older people. Work swaps became more common as neighborhoods pulled together to see everyone through. In Orange County, for example, one grower who owned a tractor "arranged to plow for some who needed plowing in the spring for work which he would need later in the summer." In other cases, teenagers and younger children jumped at the opportunity to make a few dollars working in the fields. "There seemed always to be many children . . . who had only to be approached by the farmer who needed help or some one else with the offer of a little cash and they would help very willingly," one observer reported.[10]

Growers also invested in what labor-saving technologies they could obtain to mitigate the pressures of labor shortages. Demand for tractors and other equipment spiked, even as they became increasingly difficult to obtain. Farm families replaced the fire pits on their curing barns with coal- or fuel-operated stokers to eliminate the need to cut wood all winter. Others turned to the chemical defoliants and insecticides extension agents introduced to save the time it took to chop weeds and kill pests by hand. One farm woman, overjoyed at her husband's choice to try a chemical to control weeds in the seedbed, explained that it "looks like a blessing to us women. The Lord knows I ain't getting any younger, and weeding a plant bed sure gives my bones a fit." Labor-saving tools were a boon in many ways, but they also introduced new technological dependencies that reshaped tobacco agriculture for decades to come.[11]

Families also turned to government agencies for help in securing farm labor. The nation itself, they reminded their leaders, had an important stake in making sure they could find enough labor. "I want to know how we can grow more food for the government [when] all of our boys are being drafted into the Army," asked one farmer shortly after the United States entered the war. In response to such pressure, local extension offices helped recruit workers. In Surry County, North Carolina, the local agent organized "labor registrations" at the county's schools in order to find workers. "Every boy and girl who would accept a job on a farm in Surry County was asked to register." According to the agent, organizing the students in this way was a resounding success. "Several farmers reported that they harvested their tobacco and peach crops almost entirely by going to town each morning, loading up with boys and girls, taking them out to work and taking them back at night." In Davidson County, the agent reported similar success in coordinating Victory Farm Workers with local growers. "The Workers enabled the farmers to save hay on time, cultivate corn . . . , harvest small grain . . . , [and] harvest fall crops with as little delay as possible."[12]

Local initiatives such as these were an important source of short-term labor, but they could not solve the season-long labor needs of farming families. Of the seventy-two workers the Halifax County, Virginia, extension agent placed with farmers in 1943, for example, only twelve worked for more than a month; the others helped only during the harvest. While he had been able to place ten state prisoners on farms for the summer, there simply was not enough labor willing to work long term on the farms, at least not for the wages farmers could or would pay.[13]

The problem of getting sufficient farm labor was not, of course, unique to the Old Bright Belt or even the tobacco belts as a whole. While tobacco farmers may have needed laborers for longer periods of time than other growers, farmers nationwide bemoaned their inability to attract a stable labor force. In 1942, the federal government signed a bilateral agreement with Mexico that established a program that sent Mexican laborers to come to the United States to alleviate labor shortages in California. The success of the *bracero* program led farmers along the eastern seaboard to press for the expansion of the program. In March 1943, Congress passed the Farm Labor Supply Appropriation Act, which authorized local extension agents to coordinate farm labor supply with the newly created War Food Administration's labor division. This wartime program's primary mission was to meet labor demands by matching the available domestic labor with demand. However, the act also provided for the employment of German prisoners of war and the importation of offshore workers from the Caribbean to supplement—and in many cases supplant—the nation's existing migrant agricultural labor force.[14]

Some Old Bright Belt families found workers with the help of Uncle Sam. Extension agents arranged to have both German POWs and Bahamians work for landowners in a number of counties. Large landowners who typically relied on sharecroppers were eager to have these workers. In Caswell County, where sharecropping families traditionally worked more than half the farms, landowners complained about the exodus of sharecroppers and the shortage of workers who could replace them. "It was impossible to get any migratory labor," the county extension agent reported in 1944, adding that because the county was "strictly rural, there were not any part time laborers" available from the region's towns and cities. In 1945, the extension agent secured forty-six Bahamian workers at the request of fourteen county growers in addition to a number of German prisoners of war. The next year, thirty-two farmers sought the help of the extension agent, who was able to secure fifty-eight laborers. "From July 26 to August 28 these Bahamians worked approximately 1000 man days in the harvesting of tobacco," he reported. "This extra labor was highly beneficial to the farmers using it."[15]

While finding workers was difficult, those who could grow a crop found the war years to be a time of prosperity. In Danville, prices nearly doubled during the war. Wartime rationing limited the translation of these high prices into consumer goods, but many farmers paid off debts, purchased land, and improved what they could around the farm. "From all indications farmers are not spending as much money unwisely this year as compared with the first war period," one extension agent reported, proudly noting that many of the black farmers he worked with "will receive a clear title or deed to their farm that they never dreamed of so soon from the sale of tobacco this year." High prices obviated the need for parity payments; price ceilings, in fact, replaced price floors.[16]

High prices continued into the postwar years. In the Federal Tobacco Program, farm families, it seemed, had found the right formula for prosperity. "The returning veteran along with [the] good price tobacco has paid has roped in some of our 'Land Happy' speculators, as well as some of our land cramped farmers," one black extension agent reported, adding that a number of the growers he worked with had been able to purchase substantial tracts of land. Between 1940 and 1950, the number of owner-operated farms increased by almost 10 percent, even as the total number of farms declined.[17]

The expansion of farm ownership, however, masked further disruptions to traditional labor arrangements. Larger landowners who relied on tenants found themselves pinched by the shortage of people willing to rent on shares that was attributable to outmigration. "Wages has got so high that it is hard for farmers to get tenants to work the land anymore," complained North Carolinian W. C. Gentry. Replacing croppers with wage workers was difficult because growers had to compete with the growing textile and tobacco industries for workers. Small farmers, too, faced the problem of losing their workforce as their children grew up and took jobs in town or, as a product of their parents' increasing success, went to college.[18]

As they had done during the war, many families turned to technology. In those heady years when wartime discoveries offered promises of a rich future, agricultural scientists worked hard to convince farm families to adopt numerous technologies. In the early 1950s, the American Tobacco Company, hoping to convince farmers to adopt the latest techniques to improve the tobacco they brought to market, touted the technologies being released by corporate and government engineers: new hybrids designed to resist disease; new machines to ease the work of planting, transplanting, and harvest; and the latest miracles of chemistry to protect the precious leaves from cankerous fungi and ravenous pests. "DDT is used for flea beetles, midge larvae, budworms, and cutworms, parathion for flea beetles, midge larvae, aphids, and suckflies; TEPP [tetraethyl pyrophosphate] for aphids and suckflies; TDE [tetrachloro dephenyl ethane] and endrine for hornworms; and chlordane for wireworms and grasshoppers,"one advertisement explained. As these tools replaced hand labor, they introduced new dangers, including acute poisoning.[19]

Despite the monetary and human costs, farm families began to see mechanization and chemicals use as necessities. Yet these technologies undermined the tobacco program that was keeping families afloat. The Federal Tobacco Program attempted to match production to forecasted demand. Since the Agricultural Adjustment Act measured production acres, federal administrators based their calculation of what they expected the average acre could produce. Increasing yields, however, wreaked havoc on their formulas. By the early 1960s, it was not uncommon for an acre of farmland to produce 2,000 pounds of tobacco; that same acre might have strained to produce half as much a generation earlier. Federal administrators could respond only by cutting acreage allotments. Cuts had to be ratified by farmers through referenda, but few were willing to risk an unchecked market. In 1955, growers accepted a 12 percent reduction for the 1956–1958 crops. The following year Secretary of Agriculture Ezra Taft Benson used his authority to order an immediate 20 percent reduction for the 1957 crop. Significant cuts in allotted acreage drove more people out farming.[20]

For many, like the larger growers represented by the Farm Bureau, putting up with deep cuts was simply the price of keeping the tobacco program and its guarantee of parity prices in place. Sharecroppers bore the brunt of the cuts. By 1960, the federal census had stopped counting them altogether. Small landowners faced the special problem of having sunk costs in their farms and equipment. One Virginia farmer, for example, found his nearly nine-acre allotment cut in half in just over a decade. His remaining 4.37 acres, he explained, was "not enough to make a living and to keep up the expenses on the farm." A North Carolina grower with a wife and four children wrote that he had "only 77/100 acreage" and asked "why the tobacco allotments can't be given to the farm familys [sic] that need them to make a living."[21]

Farm incomes lagged and thousands of allotted acres went unplanted as growers simply gave up. In 1950, Orange County resident H. A. Bennett complained that the county was "loosing [sic] acreage yearly" because "acreage allotments are so small" that farmers were being "forced out." In 1953, over a fifth of Forsyth County's landowners with allotments left their land completely unplanted, and the situation was similar in other counties with ready access to public work. A 1959 study found that over 10 percent of the allotments in North Carolina's Old Bright Belt counties had gone unplanted. In

1957, the Lunenburg County Extension Service agent reported that 5 percent of the county's tobacco allotment had been placed in the Soil Bank after a 20 percent allotment cut had "left a large number of our growers with less than two acres of tobacco." The number of Old Bright Belt farm operators decreased by over 40 percent in the two decades following World War II. One researcher argued that of those who remained, "a high proportion . . . would fall into the poverty category" without public work to subsidize their farming operations.[22]

The Federal Tobacco Program proved to be a mixed blessing for black farmers. For many, a tobacco allotment proved to be a saving grace. Studies of black Piedmont farmers found that allotments were a key determinant in whether black farmers remained on the land. Yet because blacks tended to own smaller tobacco farms and depend almost entirely on their tobacco crops, they experienced the dispossession of allotment reductions disproportionately. "Tobacco allotment too small," an activist working among black farmers in southern Virginia noted in 1968 noted briefly. "Afraid of the future. Picture looks worse and worse." Outright discrimination was also a serious problem. Acting through elected local committees, white elites made decisions about how allotments were distributed and enforced. Racism, as historian Pete Daniel has shown, was endemic in the system. "I own 232 ½ acres of land," one black farmer from eastern North Carolina wrote to the secretary of agriculture in 1959. "My *tobacco acreage allotment* however is 4 $^5/100$ [4.05] acres. I definitely feel I am being discriminated against by the local office of the commodity stabilization in this matter because I am a negro." Many black landowners in the Old Bright Belt doubtless shared his complaint.[23]

Acreage reductions drove more families, white and black, into part-time farming. In 1954, nearly a quarter of the farm families in North Carolina's northern Piedmont counties earned more money off the farm than on. "The importance of off-farm work," one study explained, "indicates that many families have been able to secure larger family incomes by combining farm and nonfarm work." Expanded off-farm employment among male farmers (nearly 40 percent of whom worked off the farm at some point in the year) was responsible for much of the growth in part-time farming, but women and children continued to employ diverse strategies for participation in public work. Often only one parent or older children took public work while the other parent remained on the farm. In 1958, the Davidson County extension agent reported that a number of farmers in his county "have gone to work in local industries and are leaving the tobacco crop to the rest of the family with their help after working hours and on the weekends." By the mid-1960s, more than four-fifths of Old Bright Belt farm operators reported that either they or one of their family members contributed to the household economy with income from nonfarm work.[24]

Support for the Federal Tobacco Program remained high, however. Old Bright Belt farmers pleaded with their representatives and senators to defend it, which they did from leadership positions on key congressional committees. Tobacco-state politicians chaired the House Committee on Agriculture eighteen of the twenty-four years from 1940 to 1964; North Carolina's Harold Cooley—"the best friend tobacco ever had," supportive farmers and warehousemen called him—held the position for twelve years. In addition, members of Congress from North Carolina, Virginia, and Kentucky dominated subcommittees dedicated to tobacco issues on the agriculture committees in both the House and the Senate.[25]

When Republican Secretary of Agriculture Ezra Taft Benson called for the elimination of farm subsidies aimed at the program, farm families and political leaders circled the wagons. Benson argued that such programs were counterproductive and could no longer be justified. After bruising battles over food and cotton crops, he turned his attention to the tobacco program. He first used his power as secretary to institute acreage reductions as part of a larger reduction in all crop subsidies. He was happy when corn growers abandoned production controls in 1958, and declared that tobacco and wheat would be next in line for reform or even elimination. The tobacco program caused growers to "lose markets abroad" by "pricing them out of the market," he said, and indicated that he was planning to propose lower price supports. In 1960, he revealed the purpose of his proposed reductions: to convince farmers of the need to eliminate production controls entirely. Speaking before reporters, Benson made it clear that "it was time for 90 percent support level [of parity] on tobacco to be broken and for acreage to be expanded so that this country [can] regain its position in the world market." It was time, in other words, for the Federal Tobacco Program to be dismantled.[26]

Farmers and their political allies disagreed. Although they complained loudly about acreage cuts, they continued to support the program overwhelmingly. In 1958, just as Benson hoped to begin cutting the tobacco program, more than 95 percent of flue-cured growers approved the continuation of the program. The deepest wells of support were in the Old Bright Belt. When Benson announced his desire to see production controls lifted in 1960, Democrats used his opposition to the program to rally farmers against the

Republican Party as it tried to leverage President Eisenhower's popularity to win the Upper South for Richard Nixon. Campaigning for the Democratic Party in Rocky Mount, North Carolina, Harry S. Truman reminded tobacco farmers that Benson "would have ruined" them without Democrats' efforts to "keep his hands tied" regarding the tobacco program.[27]

Benson was wrong on the politics, but he was right that federal agricultural programs, including the Federal Tobacco Program, faced steep challenges. The Commodity Credit Corporation was spending millions on commodity programs in wheat, corn, and other food crops and amassing surpluses that could not be disposed of. . The Federal Tobacco Program was healthier, in large part because of stringent production controls, but leaf was piling up. While Stabilization initially was largely successful in reselling the tobacco it purchased, in the late 1950s the program found it more difficult to locate buyers. By 1959, only 28.3 percent of the program's 1955 stocks and 43.7 percent of its 1956 stocks had been sold, and most of the 1957 crop sat in storage awaiting buyers. The fate of the 1958 crop was no better: only 2.7 percent had moved in the five months it had been up for sale. Stabilization's inability to move the stored tobacco took its toll on the cooperative's finances. By 1959, it owed the Commodity Credit Corporation nearly $372 million in principal alone (about 37.5 percent of the money it had borrowed since 1946) and over $11 million in carrying charges for tobacco in storage. Since farmers received their funds from Stabilization as "non-recourse" loans (loans that did not have to be paid back), they did not feel the pain. Stabilization's managers did. Stabilization was not in immediate danger, general manager L. T. Weeks said publicly in June of 1959, but it had reached a "crossroads" that demanded "some careful and sound thinking."[28]

Much of the problem, Weeks explained, was the large volume of poor-quality leaves that Stabilization was obligated by law to purchase but buyers were uninterested in purchasing, even at deeply discounted prices. "It is a recognizable fact that much of the tobacco Stabilization holds in its inventory is classified as undesirable." Growers, he claimed, had become so used to the fact that all of their tobacco would sell that they no longer had any incentive to grow high-quality tobacco. He cited five sources of poor-quality tobacco: production focused on volume rather than quality; unmarketable tobacco varieties; poor cultural practices; the use of unapproved chemicals; and poor preparation of product for the market. He pleaded with growers to improve their work, warning that the program could not "continue in its present form on a sound basis" unless the problems were corrected.[29]

Stabilization was in a difficult bind. Although it carried out federal policy, as a growers' cooperative it did not have the authority to compel growers to make any changes. Such compulsory measures had to come from the federal government. But even the government's options were limited. Little could be done to force growers to change their growing techniques. Extension Service agents might plead with growers to give attention to quality, but in an era of declining allotments and a tight labor market, most growers felt little compunction about growing as much as they could as efficiently as they could do it. Even Weeks had to admit that the pressures on farmers to bring yields up were great. "Increased yields per acre have been made possible with more 'know-how,' new varieties and research information. I have no quarrel with this. A tobacco grower who has not increased his yield per acre since the tobacco program has been in effect has either been a poor manager or has experienced extremely adverse conditions."[30]

The least painful solution was to stop forcing Stabilization to take in the kind of leaf that would not sell. To do this, federal regulators devised the Variety Discount Program. Introduced in 1957, the program gave Stabilization the ability to limit its liability on less-desirable varieties of tobacco by paying only 50 percent of parity. The goal of the program was to force growers to stop using varieties manufacturers clearly did not want. A number of varieties were placed to the list initially and more were added later, most because some quality in the leaf, often low nicotine content, had appeared during manufacturing that led cigarette makers to reject it.

The Variety Discount Program marked an important shift in the federal government's position in the tobacco economy. For the first time, the state used its power to define the market's standards, not simply describe them. By defining certain varieties as unacceptable, the federal government forced growers to change their practices virtually overnight. Like the tobacco program as a whole, force came in the form of severe disincentives, not coerced mandates. As the program evolved, it expanded to cover not only undesirable varieties but also certain grades of tobacco that Stabilization found hard to resell. In time, support for certain varieties and grades was dropped entirely.

Growers' responses to the new mandates varied. Switching varieties caused some discomfort for growers who had adopted varieties affected by the program in order to increase yields, reduce labor requirements, or combat various plant diseases. Coker 139, Coker 140, and Dixie Bright 244, three of the first varieties put on the discount list, had high yields; were designed to resist black shank and Granville wilt; flowered late—meaning the leaves had more time to grow; and produced fewer suckers. When these varieties were released for planting in 1955, they appeared to be the solution to many problems growers experienced. All three had comparatively low nicotine levels, however, which made them undesirable to manufacturers who were attempting to increase the nicotine content of their cigarettes. Fortunately for growers, new breeds that were acceptable to manufacturers quickly replaced the discounted varieties, making the pain of the discount program only temporary.[31]

A more daunting problem for Stabilization arose in the late 1950s: the use of maleic hydrazide on tobacco. Farmers used the chemical to control sucker growth on plants in the fields, but tobacco companies claimed that it damaged the leaves to the point that they could not use them in their products. They pressed farmers to stop using it and refused to buy treated leaf from Stabilization. Ultimately, they sought to ban it. But they could not use the Federal Tobacco Program to control farmers' choices.

Maleic hydrazide, commonly called MH-30 after the popular version marketed by the Uniroyal Chemical Company, was first formulated in the late nineteenth century. In the 1940s, scientists discovered its usefulness as a growth inhibitor. It was considered to be a safe compound; it supposedly posed a hazard to humans only in large doses and had little long-term impact on the environment. In the early 1950s, Extension Service agents introduced it to tobacco farmers, who soon found it to be irreplaceable. Hard-pressed growers latched on to the new chemical as a way of maintaining the quality of their crops without having to find the labor to remove suckers by hand. By the early 1960s, as one North Carolina grower explained, most farm families relied on the chemical. "If you told me to go anywhere flue-cured tobacco is grown in this country to find a grower that does not use MH-30, I wouldn't know where to find him." Spray-happy farmers followed the old dictum that if a little was good, a lot was better, prompting some Extension Service agents to call it "MH-90."[32]

Extension Service agents initially greeted growers' rapid adoption of MH-30 with joy, but their excitement faded when cigarette manufacturers declared that they had no interest in buying leaves treated with MH-30. "Cigarette companies and [tobacco] dealers," the New York Times put it, "like MH-30 as much as Carrie Nation liked a good sipping whisky." Manufacturers complained that the chemical damaged the leaves, making them "heavier, slicker, and harder to blend" with untreated leaves. Beyond physical appearances, they argued, MH-30 knocked the sugar-nicotine ratio out of balance, which "adversely affect[ed] the flavor and aroma" and reduced the "filling power" of the leaves (a measure of the amount of tobacco needed to make a cigarette). British manufacturers' disapproval of the product, in fact, led to an early ban on the use of MH-30 on flue-cured tobacco in Canada and Southern Rhodesia; the ban also led American tobacco companies to look to these countries for leaf free of MH-30. Unable to prompt a similar ban in the United States, manufacturers instructed buyers to avoid any crop that was determined to have been treated with the chemical.[33]

By the late 1950s, Stabilization found itself burdened with tons of tobacco treated with MH-30 that it could not sell at any price. In 1959, general manager L. T. Weeks complained that the treated leaf placed undue burdens on the program. He told stockholders that "regardless of the advantages from the use of MH-30, . . . it is a fact that [its] use . . . caused many millions of pounds of tobacco to come into the inventory of Stabilization from the 1958 crops which would have otherwise gone into trade channels." "To date," he continued, "not the first pound of this tobacco has been sold and no interest has been shown in it whatsoever."[34]

In a free market, buyers' refusal to buy leaf treated with MH-30 would have forced a rapid decline in use of the product. However, growers had a buyer of last resort in Stabilization. E. Y. Floyd, director of the Plant Food Institute of North Carolina and Virginia, a fertilizer industry group, explained the power this gave growers. If buyers did not want tobacco treated with MH-30, he wrote to Joe R. Williams, director of the Agricultural Stabilization and Conservation Service's Tobacco Division, "there positively will have to be prohibitive legislation to keep the people from using it. After this market year there is no way in the world that any agency in this State could prevent it from being used."[35]

In fact, both manufacturers and Stabilization pursued such legal prohibitions. Banning maleic hydrazide outright was improbable given its use in controlling bud growth on stored potatoes, so they looked to the Variety Discount Program to find ways to curtail its use. Adding any varieties to the discount program required congressional approval, though, and those pushing for action found little support on Capitol Hill. In 1960, the Tobacco Subcommittee of the House Agriculture Committee held hearings on MH-30 but concluded by directing the USDA to study the problem further. The following year, the USDA produced a study that supported the claims of manufacturers: MH-30 affected leaf color, altered the chemical composition of the leaves, offered a number of challenges to manufacturing, reduced filling capacity, and adversely affected taste. Nevertheless, the USDA ruled out proscribing MH-30 because a ban would irreparably hurt growers. Unwilling to offend either growers or manufacturers, the USDA offered only a weak recommendation: an "expanded research program should be developed to find methods of sucker control acceptable to both farmers and industry."[36]

USDA officials understood that limiting the use of MH-30 would place growers in a bind by forcing them to return to hand-suckering. Congress also heard growers' voices on the matter and refused to upset this constituency. "Don't let them outlaw MH 30 on tobacco," was one grower's concise message to North Carolina Old Bright Belt member of Congress Horace Kornegay in 1962. Member of Congress Harold Cooley reported that he "received dozens of communications opposing outlawing" MH-30. "I have not received a single communication from a tobacco farmer which opposes the use of this labor saving chemical."[37]

MH-30 rekindled farm families' old animosities toward the tobacco companies. One anonymous writer argued that it was the chemical's potential to cause a "reduction in filling capacity" that worried buyers, not its effects on taste or aroma. Their talk about quality, he argued, was just a cover for their fear that "it may require more tobacco to make the same amount of cigarettes," forcing them to buy more from growers. Charges that manufacturers wanted to buy even less must have resonated with growers already hurt in the late 1950s by reductions in tobacco usage caused by the addition of filter tips, which reduced the volume of tobacco in each cigarette by roughly a quarter. North Carolina grower John C. Williamson argued that tobacco companies' "high profits and large dividends" should bear the costs of this "adjustment" in demand and not make things harder on farm families.[38]

Many farm families also took accusations of damaged leaves personally. They knew tobacco, they said, and, like generations before them, claimed expertise based on their work in the fields and barns. "I defy . . . any living man to make a positive identification or selection of MH-30 treated tobacco and hand-suckered tobacco in its cured stage," John Williamson challenged MH-30's opponents. To accuse a family of taking shortcuts was deeply insulting and reminded some of decades of buyers' complaints that growers produced too much low-quality tobacco. Growers' letters seethed with resentment. One North Carolina grower taunted cigarette makers with their own slogans. Manufacturers, he wrote, "complain and depress the [market] [by] always talking about quality being inferior, but when they are selling it[']s quite a different story. 'It's the tobacco end that counts,' 'Golden rich mellow tobaccos,' 'Tobacco too good to filter,' and so it goes, they all have their slogans. They don't tell them it's the same tobacco with MH 30 or disc[ount] variety not even to say anything about the stems or floor sweepings. I believe anyone can see it's the same old trick of the trade used all down through the ages." Another grower wrote, "We all know that these companies showed remarkable ingenuity in accommodating their blending processes to the use of 're-constituted' or 'homogenized' tobacco (stem materials, sweepings, etc. which were formerly thrown away but which now make up a sizable per cent of some cigarettes)."[39]

The responses of farm families to manufacturers' complaints about MH-30 also betrayed insecurities about the pace of change. The sea change in tobacco agriculture generated anxiety. One county Extension Service agent picked up on growers' frustration. Despite rising prices, he reported, "there is some question in the minds of many of our good tobacco farmers as to the quality of the crop as a whole." To many, quality "doesn't mean the same as it did in years past," in large part because of the new technologies and techniques farmers had to adopt to keep up. One grower was dissatisfied with the variety of tobacco he planted, despite the fact that it garnered more than $1,400 per acre, "because the quality of the tobacco did not measure up to his idea of what quality should be." This grower was not alone; "many . . . good tobacco farmers" were also "interested and concerned about these things."[40]

Congress never took action to limit the use of MH-30. Instead, the issue became one for the agro-industrial complex to resolve bureaucratically. In 1964, cigarette companies, chemical companies, and the USDA formed the Sucker Control Advisory Committee to craft a solution. The committee's membership and research program alike reflected the corporate-state cooperation that increasingly precluded grower participation in the development of agricultural policy in the second half of the twentieth century. The committee was composed of representatives of the largest U.S. cigarette manufacturers, the Imperial Tobacco Company of the United Kingdom, companies that made MH-30 and similar chemicals, and state and federal agencies. Numerous tests of various chemicals were run at state experiment stations, and industry scientists evaluated the results. The committee never recommended an outright ban on MH-30. Manufacturers made it clear that they preferred farmers not use the chemical, but they realized they lacked the political clout to force even a bureaucratic change.[41]

In the late 1960s, the debate over MH-30 took an abrupt turn when questions about the safety of the chemical emerged. In 1967, already confronted with growing evidence of the link between smoking and cancer, manufacturers responded with alarm when they received news that a researcher was planning to release a report that indicated that MH-30 led to the development of tumors in newborn mice. The last thing they wanted was a link to cancer for a chemical that was widely used on tobacco. British buyers, who were trying desperately to overturn their country's ban on chemically treated leaf, worried that the study results would wreck any chance that the restrictions would be loosened. American buyers worried too. "Although everyone there seemed to recognize the magnitude of the problem, no one seemed to know what, if any, actions could be taken," reported one person who attended the April 1967 meeting of the Sucker Control Committee meeting. "If a carcinogenic potential for a substance is 'hinted' even in some obscure experiments on mammals," an American Tobacco Company researcher warned in a confidential memo, "the usual Federal Governmental Action is to declare a zero-tolerance for that substance 'pending clarification' of the possible implications . . . for man." Manufacturers did not want their products held up because of questions about MH-30.[42]

Instead of using the pending report as an opportunity to push for a ban on MH-30, tobacco companies did their best to continue the pattern of obfuscation they had perfected in their efforts to discredit studies that linked tobacco to disease. Shortly after the report on MH-30 appeared in the journal *Nature*, the Tobacco Institute's public relations firm issued a press release that questioned the research model by noting that "despite a high incidence of tumors in the experimental mice, no pulmonary carcinomas were found," concluding that "this would seem to cast some doubt on the significance of MH-30 on tobacco for human beings." Tobacco companies may have had their doubts about MH-30, but they stopped calling for the end to its use.[43]

In 1964, the release of the surgeon general's report *Smoking and Health* initiated a change in the relationship between growers and manufacturers. By the late 1960s, both were facing uncertain times, and each provided something the other needed. Tobacco companies needed a human face to make their products defensible, and growers needed political clout in the face of increasing hostility toward their crops and the programs that made it possible to grow them for a profit.

6

Untied

On January 11, 1964, U.S. surgeon general Luther Terry altered the history of tobacco forever when he released *Smoking and Health*, a comprehensive analysis of studies of tobacco consumption that linked smoking to a host of health problems, including lung cancer. The national media offered multi-page coverage of the release, taking care to interview tobacco industry representatives, who rushed to call the report into question. But local media in tobacco-growing regions barely took note of the report. The *Danville Register* focused on the record snowstorm that hit the city that January. The *Winston-Salem Journal* said that the report garnered little more than "shrug" from the "man in the street." Old Bright Belt farm families also took a wait-and-see attitude. "It's definitely going to have its effect," a member of the Virginia Bright Flue-Cured Tobacco Commission counseled. "It's going to hurt our industry . . . but we'll come out of it. I'm confident of that." And they were right, at least in the short term. Cigarette sales dropped some in 1964, but 1965 sales reached record levels, and smoking rates held nearly constant into the early 1970s. *Smoking and Health* may have led some individuals and families to contemplate the cancer-causing plants in their fields, but they did not need to take a side in the cigarette wars for another decade.[1]

More important to the work of farm families was a 1968 change in the rules for marketing tobacco. That year, federal regulators decided to allow Old Bright Belt farmers to sell their tobacco on the auction floors without first tying it into hands. The change altered the market overnight. "No one is interested in tied tobacco when most of the offerings are in the untied form," one buyer explained. By the 1970s, very few families spent the autumn days skillfully tying tobacco. Instead, they piled it on drop cloths or, more often, dumped it into balers that turned out unremarkable cubes of leaf.[2]

The new sales method drove the widespread adoption of two new tools: the mechanical harvester and the bulk curing barn. Both had been invented before the policy change but had proven impractical as long as farm families needed to make hands. Harvesters tore the leaves from the plants, often leaving the axil behind, and bulk curing barns, long metal sheds into which farmers slid metal racks filled with leaves, required farmers to fasten the leaves to small metal posts that left holes in the leaves. Hands made from these leaves would have been a sorry sight, and farm families continued to rely on older methods. Once the policy change made the last manual task obsolete, the road to mechanization and modernization was wide open. Farm families adapted, but with misgivings.[3]

By the 1970s, the tobacco economy was at a turning point. Mechanization, the expansion of bright tobacco agriculture to other parts of the world, changes in demand, and, most ominous, an increase in opposition to tobacco in the public sphere forced every sector of the American tobacco economy to adjust. As farm families made the necessary changes, the culture of farming bright tobacco changed. When machines replaced manual tasks, women and children left the fields and male farmers became managers who oversaw the waged laborers who operated the machines. The world of family farming that bright tobacco had made came undone.

It is a commonplace to equate the transformation of twentieth-century southern agriculture with mechanization. It is far more complex than that, but the change does start there. New tools designed to make agriculture more efficient flooded the southern countryside in the decades following World War II. While the Old Bright Belt was perhaps not as reshaped as places such as the Mississippi delta, it still was part of a technological revolution. Beginning in the late 1940s, new technologies aimed at simplifying or eliminating tasks that government and industry experts identified as inefficient emerged from university, government, and tobacco-industry laboratories. Greenhouses replaced seedbeds, obviating the need to dig, burn, and tend new beds every year. Tractor-pulled mechanical transplanters replaced the hand techniques that had taken so much time in earlier years. Instead of hauling plants and water to the fields, workers rode through the fields, dropping plants into a machine that placed them at preset intervals and doused them with the proper amount of water. In time, machines that were more automated replaced these manually operated implements. Chemical defoliants and pesticides removed the need for the tasks of hoeing, worming, and suckering. Mechanical harvesters, the earliest of which were simply tractors that drove workers through the fields at just the right height to prime leaves as they passed, came along slowly but steadily. So did bulk barns, the first of which engineers developed in the 1950s. Within a generation, the most labor-intensive crop was becoming one of the most capital-intensive crops.[4]

Designed to make work easier for farm families, the new tools actually undermined the need for family workers. Child workers remained common well into the 1980s, but their work did not stretch through the summers as it once had. Women disappeared from the fields and especially the barns at an increasing rate, except on the smallest farms. In the 1950s, engineers introduced looping machines designed to reduce the time women spent tying small bundles of leaves to the sticks that were used to hang them in the curing barns. When bulk curing came along, this task was eliminated altogether. No longer did girls carefully hand up leaves for tying; no longer did mothers spend long hours sorting and tying their money crop. Instead, more and more women took off-farm work to support their husbands' efforts to run the farms.

Even with machines, tobacco farming still required long hours of back-breaking work, but these hours were increasingly concentrated in the harvest season. A few workers could handle the average farm most of the year, but, as one expert explained, "assembling large harvest crews needed only for a few weeks during harvest became more and more of a problem for tobacco growers." One farmer put it more simply: "People want steady work, they don't care about pullin' 'bacca." Another complained, "Field hands is going at two dollars, two fifty an hour. Field hands! And at that price we can't find enough of 'em around." Growers found it harder to secure traditional sources of extra labor—extended family and neighbors—to see them through. By the mid-1960s, three-quarters of Virginia and North Carolina tobacco farms employed some sort of seasonal labor, usually migrant laborers moving up the eastern seaboard, but this was most concentrated largely in eastern North Carolina, where the consolidation of allotments by large landowners had pushed thousands of sharecroppers to the cities.[5]

Old Bright Belt growers adjusted to seasonal migrant farm labor more slowly. Up into the 1970s, the Piedmont, unlike the coastal plain, still had a sizable rural workforce and growers retained a greater ability to find labor from the cities during the peak weeks of the harvest, often with the help of government. In 1964, Halifax County growers resuscitated the practice of having county officials recruit teenagers from town to get enough labor for the fields. Growers in neighboring Mecklenburg went so far as to import teenagers from outside the county through a state program that was beneficial to all involved, at least according to state officials. "We were able to supply our tobacco growers with a much needed labor supply, but more than that, a group of teenagers were trained in accepting responsibilities of work and earned a considerable amount of money to help defray the expenses of the coming school year," state officials reported. As late as 1974, some Wake County, North Carolina, school districts delayed the opening of schools to adjust for a late harvest. "For the last three years, the farmers could not have harvested the crops without school kids," said the county extension agent, explaining the delay. In many cases, these students were not even the children of tobacco growers, but neighborhood kids drawn by the relatively good wages. One farmer said, "T'want for the kids, don't know how we'd git it outta the field."[6]

Hiring high schoolers worked for many small growers, but larger, specialized growers demanded a more reliable and, in their minds, more controllable workforce. "I have an interest in a tobacco farm in Person County . . . and it is getting impossible to lease or rent tobacco acreage profitably . . . due to the scarcity of farmers and farm labor," complained one landowner. Larger growers increasingly sought to attract migrant workers. North Carolina officials dated the use of migrant workers in the Piedmont to the few that worked the fields in the early 1970s. By 1976, they estimated that 1,500 migrants were at work in the fields of the state's central Piedmont counties. Most of the workers were young Latino men.[7]

Differences in ethnicity and language compounded the workers' status as outsiders and highlighted the shift away from the region's family- and community-based labor networks. Some growers attempted to make adjustments in order to work with the migrants, perhaps with some hope of recreating the region's traditional personalized labor relations. A few Yadkin County, North Carolina, growers signed up for Spanish classes "to learn to work with the Puerto Ricans and Mexicans on their farms." On most farms, however, labor relations became increasingly depersonalized as growers simply relied on the crew leaders that brought the workers north from Florida to communicate their instructions.[8]

The reliance on crew leaders demonstrated the extent to which tobacco labor had become loosed from its familial moorings. While some workers came of their own volition and others came as part of crews led by federally registered labor recruiters, most had been recruited by so-called freewheelers who lured workers with promises of good money. The entire system, especially the use of freewheelers, had a long history of abuse and fraud, and allegations of such behavior by labor contractors surfaced in the Old Bright Belt. In 1981, Caswell County authorities discovered twenty-five migrant workers living in squalor in an abandoned farmhouse on land they had been hired to work. The workers reported that the crew leader had taken a sizable portion of their pay—$20 upfront and 50 cents for each hour worked—and provided little in the way of food and shelter. They also accused the crew leader of holding them against their will. The farmer on whose land they worked protested that he had no knowledge of the conditions the workers were enduring. He lived on another farm a few miles away and said he believed the crew leader was responsible. "He seemed like a straight-forward guy. He said he had a license," the farmer told reporters. Clearly this grower had little contact with the people who were working his tobacco.[9]

By the 1980s, some farmers began to have misgivings about using migrant laborers, an increasing number of whom were undocumented Latino workers. They not only feared the legal implications of hiring so-called illegal aliens but also desired greater stability in the workforce. Increasingly, they turned to imported foreign farm laborers to work their fields. Commonly known as "H-2 workers," (so named because of the subsection of the U.S. immigration law allowing for their importation), these workers came to the United States through permits issued by the U.S. Department of Labor. Since 1952, the H-2 program had allowed the importation of seasonal farm workers from other countries (mostly from Jamaica and the Bahamas at first but later also from Mexico), but Old Bright Belt growers had not used it. Because there was a sufficient pool of local and migrant farm labor in the 1970s, they saw no need to bear the high costs of transporting and housing the workers. (Under the H-2 provision, growers have to pay the transportation costs of the workers and provide rent-free housing while they are on the farm.)

In 1980, a number of Virginia growers took the lead and began bringing in temporary farm workers, almost all from Mexico. By 1983, they were bringing in several hundred workers each year. The workers came in time for spring planting and left shortly after the autumn harvest. It was nearly another decade before growers in North Carolina's Old Bright Belt farmers began to import guest workers through the foreign labor program (known since 1986 as the H2-A program because of the recodification of the Immigration Reform and Control Act in that year). In 1989, tobacco growers statewide joined with farmers of other crops to form the North Carolina Growers Association and placed the state's first order for workers through the H-2A program. By 1997, North Carolina had become the largest user of H-2A farm labor, much of it in the tobacco fields. In 1999, a quarter of all H-2A certification permits nation-wide were given to North Carolina growers, and Virginia ranked third in the number of permits issued that year. Nationwide, work in tobacco accounted for 42 percent of all H-2A certifications, more than twice the participation of workers in the next job category, vegetable harvesting.[10]

Growers cited the decreasing availability and reliability of U.S.-based workers as the reason for the shift. They claimed that few locals were will-ing to work in the tobacco fields and that migrants were increasingly difficult to find. Pittsylvania County, Virginia, grower Tommie Willis spoke of H-2A workers as "insurance" and claimed that having them on his farm saved him the headache of recruiting enough labor for his crops. "You don't have work-ers when you need them unless you get Mexicans," he explained. Neil Jones of Brunswick County, Virginia, said similar things about foreign workers: "You don't want to come here at 5 a.m. and wonder who's going to show up. I don't know of anybody in this area who doesn't use foreign workers."[11]

Critics have pointed out that the wages that growers were willing to offer was the biggest impediment to securing workers, not dried-up labor pools. The H-2A program is a way around the labor market's own laws of supply and demand. "H-2A enables farmers—from small operators to corporate giants employing more than 600 workers—to effectively circumvent the free mar-ket, paying guestworkers as little as $6.39 an hour rather than raising hourly wages to attract U.S. workers," investigator Barry Yeoman argued in a 2001 article.[12]

Additionally, what growers call stability, critics call coercion. The H-2A program requires that workers stay with the grower the sponsoring grow-ers' agency assigns them to. If a worker leaves, he—they are almost entirely male—voids his contract and becomes an undocumented alien. (This is not to say that many do not leave; estimates of desertion rates reach almost 40 percent in some areas.) In addition, growers can send workers back for breaching their contract, a power that is ripe for abuse. Reports of workers being sent back for complaining about working conditions, wages, or inju-ries are rampant. In April 2004, farm workers sued the North Carolina Grow-ers Association for blacklisting workers who reported problems with their treatment.[13]

The growers' organizations respond that they do their best to adhere the program's requirements in the face of shifting Department of Labor policies, red tape, and, lawsuits that, according to Stan Eury, the acerbic president of the North Carolina Growers Association, are the result of "a huge conspiracy of liberal farmworker advocacy that includes litigation and media smear campaigns" against "law-abiding farmers." They claim that the system works better than the previous system of relying on migrant and undocumented workers and that the vast majority of respectable growers are made to suffer because of gross misrepresentations of the operation of the program as a whole. And, they claim, the program's guidelines ensure that workers on H-2A farms are much better off than those on unregulated farms.[14]

Many H-2A workers would beg to differ. While there are certainly some growers who are fair and build long-term relationships with workers—growers can request the workers they would like and a number of workers return to the same growers every year—evidence shows that working conditions are often unsafe, the living conditions inhumane, and the wages below the federally mandated minimum. Workers have even reported being compelled to labor in the fields at gunpoint.[15] In recent years, growers have increasingly abandoned the guest worker program, seeing it as too costly or too much to manage. Farmworker advocates report that conditions have not improved.[16]

After a century of dominance, family labor has become the exception rather than the rule in the Old Bright Belt. Large farmers who see their farms as businesses have replaced small landowning farmers and tenants who lived in the interstices that connect fields and barns and homes. The hands that have replaced theirs now come and go with the seasons via globalized labor streams. For most in the Old Bright Belt, tobacco is no longer king.

Buyout

In April 2005, dozens of people assembled in an auditorium at St. Paul's College in southern Virginia to learn about the death of the federal tobacco program. Or, more accurately, they came together for a sort of reading of the will. The federal Farm Service Agency and various growers' organizations held meetings across the Tobacco South that spring for the same purpose. The previous fall, Congress had put a clause deep in the pages of the American Jobs Creation Act of 2004 that killed the program, which had been in effect for over seventy years. The law eliminated all New Deal–era federal price-support programs for tobacco and provided more than $10 billion in compensation for growers and allotment holders. The farmers and others gathered at St. Paul's that warm spring day were there to learn how they could get their share of the payout. Trepidation, not celebration or even sorrow, permeated the meeting. Perhaps it was heightened because the meeting was called by the National Black Farmers' Association, which had recently won a lawsuit against the USDA for historical discrimination, but accounts of other meetings that spring and interviews with growers reported similar responses to the buyout, as it came to be known. "I've got more questions than answers," replied one eastern North Carolina farmer when asked to assess the buyout. "What are we going to turn to?" lamented another.[1]

Their concern was understandable. At least three generations of American tobacco farmers had come of age during the New Deal dispensation, during which farmers traded the freedom to choose how much tobacco they would grow in exchange for the relative security of guaranteed minimum prices for their crops. For over seventy years, federal controls brought relative stability to domestic tobacco markets and relative prosperity to the nation's tobacco farmers. And not just the largest and most capitalized, either; the program's production limits made it possible for many small growers to survive, if not thrive, even as consolidation squeezed out small farmers of other crops. Now, without price supports for their crops or limits on how much their larger, better-capitalized, and more mechanized neighbors could grow, small farmers simply could not stay in the business of growing tobacco. This was the logic of the buyout: pay growers something approximating the value of their allotments to help them make the transition away from tobacco. That all growers received payouts no matter what their size and many allotment-holding nongrowers would benefit were not matters of great concern to those who advocated ending the program. Despite the cost of the buyout, Senator George Allen of Virginia argued, "I believe it is fair compensation to end this government program." The trepidation growers felt in the spring of 2005 was heightened by the urgency of the changes taking place. Like family members of the deceased, they had to make decisions quickly; there would be no timed phase-out of the program and therefore little time to make plans for the future.[2]

None should have been caught unaware. Like a terminally ill patient, the tobacco program's death was not unforeseen. From its inception, the program had faced many criticisms: free marketers argued that it was an unnatural (and unnecessary) intrusion into the market; small farmers said it squeezed them too tightly, while larger ones chafed under its limits; anti-smoking advocates criticized the folly of encouraging farmers to grow a deadly product; and "good government" critics pointed to unintended consequences of the program, especially the large number of nonfarmers who made money from renting out their allotments. Since at least the 1970s, the program's demise had seemed imminent. Yet it survived, protected by friends in high places. Even as anti-smoking fervor reached a fevered pitch in the 1990s, the program survived, protected by a bipartisan assortment of well-placed tobacco-state politicians.

The death of the federal tobacco program marked the end of the long relationship between farm families and the state. It also signaled the end of family labor as the dominant method of organizing tobacco work in the Old Bright Belt. The program had been that system's life support. Without its protections, the family farm that had seemed so natural to tobacco farming in the twentieth century passed and new ways of organizing labor became most common.

As technological revolutions reshaped agricultural work in the 1970s, the logic behind the Federal Tobacco Program strained to account for new developments in the tobacco economy. Adopting new technologies pushed farm families to develop economies of scale to make their machines and labor profitable. Because of the cost, a family could no longer hope to make a good living on five acres, so they pressed for access to more allotment acreage. Before 1962, the process for getting additional allotments was haphazard, since allotments had to stay with the farm on which they had been established. After the introduction of a lease-and-transfer program that year, allotment renting increased dramatically. By 1972, about 30 percent of flue-cured allotments had been leased by one grower from another. At the same time, the number of allotment owners far outstripped the number of actual tobacco farmers. These owners—a mixed lot of part-time or retired farmers, nonfarming widows and descendants, and private companies—made up an important constituency in debates over the fate of the Federal Tobacco Program.[3]

While the ratio of owners to lessors should have created a renter's market, the fact that leases could not be made across county lines (a provision in the law designed to protect the outflow of allotments from regions where small farmers predominated) created shortages in certain counties and drove up prices. As early as 1965, leases in Guilford County, North Carolina, averaged about $150 per acre. By the early 1970s, allotment cuts made them even more valuable: bankers figured that the average allotted acre could bring $1,500 in the Piedmont. (In eastern North Carolina's coastal plain, the same allotment could bring $10,000 per year!) Commercially minded growers, especially those to the east and south of the Old Bright Belt, bemoaned the high rates, especially as some allotments remained unplanted and unleased. In response, allotment seekers (and some allotment owners, especially in counties where there were excess allotments) called for changes in the program to allow them to leases across county lines.[4]

Small growers across the Old Bright Belt responded that such a plan would undermine their operations as surely as the elimination of controls. Petitioning Congressman Ike Andrews to fight any plan to allow intercounty allotment leasing, grower Jesse Edmonds asserted that cross-county allotment leasing "would greatly hamper the efforts of the Piedmont farmers to stay in competition with the larger Eastern tobacco farmers." "If farmers from other areas are allowed to compete with us for our local poundage," he explained, "we could easily be forced out." Dozens of growers signed his letter in support. Petitions from other growers followed. Andrews responded that he would do all he could "to protect and promote the financial position of the farmers in our district," assuring Edmonds in a handwritten postscript that he knew the stakes. "I don't want all of our tobacco to move to the east, and it seems that this would likely happen." Others noted that opponents of a liberalized lease-and-transfer program were not concerned with saving their farms as much as with maintaining the tidy sums they received from lessees. "Lotsa people 'round here don't care 'bout growin' it no more," farmer Ralph Daniels explained. "Just wanna keep their lease money up."[5]

The evolving tobacco economy placed Old Bright Belt growers in a difficult bind with regard to the Federal Tobacco Program. All recognized its historical importance, but its ability to stabilize the market was growing increasingly shaky. The 1970s was a rough decade for growers all around, but Old Bright Belt growers felt especially vulnerable. Inflation and high energy prices drove up production costs, while increased competition from foreign countries eroded the global market share of U.S. growers. In 1975, Ike Andrews reported that growers in his district were "extremely frustrated and dissatisfied" because of low prices, increased quotas (meaning more tobacco was coming to market), and the volume of tobacco going into Stabilization (and thus earning farmers only parity prices). "We the farmers of [Virginia] are losing money, by the increase of products & labor to raise the tobacco with," one grower wrote. "This year I have payed [sic] double to raise my crop that is not as large as I have had." The problems increasingly divided growers into two camps: those who wanted to maintain the program and its traditional protections and those who were interested in reforms that would allow growers to compete internationally.[6]

In 1972 and 1973, Secretary of Agriculture Earl Butz responded to calls for greater liberalization of the program by implementing 10 percent increases in tobacco allotments. The move was quietly cheered by some larger growers and tobacco companies, some of which had proposed the expansion as a response to the high tobacco prices of the early 1970s. The Old Bright Belt's small growers, however, voiced great fear about the changes. Responding to their fears, Representative Charlie Rose, whose district included many small farmers in eastern North Carolina and who was seen statewide as a true champion of the Federal Tobacco Program's support for small growers, publicly accused the USDA of manipulating the program to the detriment of his state's farmers.[7]

In December 1973, however, Butz went further and suggested that production controls be eliminated entirely on the 1974 crop, despite the fact that growers had already voted to adhere to the increased limits. Butz said that parity prices would remain, but the controls would not. His idea was to increase the U.S. market share in a bid to weaken the power of non-U.S. growers, but small Old Bright Belt growers believed that his goal was to fatally weaken the Federal Tobacco Program at the behest of tobacco companies.

Growers and allotment owners of all stripes made it clear that they were not interested in killing the Federal Tobacco Program and rallied to stop Butz. Across the Tobacco South, growers' organizations petitioned local, state, and federal politicians, who, in turn, passed numerous resolutions calling on Butz to make a public statement that backed away from what he had said. Old Bright Belt growers wrote angry, terrified letters to their representatives and senators. "I am afraid the price of tobacco will get so cheap that we can't make a living and pay our taxes on our land," one grower wrote. Without production controls, another said, "I will be forced to quit farming and seek public employment." A Danville widow who was dependent on her allotment rental for income expressed fear as well: "If this is done, many farmers would be ruined, and especially those in the Old Belt market. With the program in effect the Old Belt has a problem of getting buyers. If controls are lifted, the tobacco companies would fill their orders down South, and the market here would suffer greatly, and I believe, eventually be eliminated."[8]

The activism worked and Butz stepped back. In 1975, he even implemented a 15 percent allotment reduction in response to changed market conditions. The challenge he posed to the program revealed the extent to which growers still saw the Federal Tobacco Program as a critical piece of the tobacco economy. Growers revealed they still believed the state had a role in not only regulating the market but also in maintaining the support for small growers that had long undergirded its popularity.

However, growers feared that state support for their work was becoming less sure. In the 1970s, anti-tobacco initiatives became more numerous and more effective as the link between cancer and smoking became more widely accepted. As some political leaders from outside the Tobacco South began to question whether the government should be in the business of underwriting a cancer-causing crop, pro-tobacco politicians avoided serious discussion of the Federal Tobacco Program lest they provide an opportunity for anti-tobacco legislators to weaken it. In the wake of one tough legislative struggle, North Carolina representative L. H. Fountain put it bluntly: "We're not finding it as easy as we used to to find support for the tobacco farmer."[9]

President Jimmy Carter's nomination of Joseph Califano as secretary of the Department of Health, Education, and Welfare (HEW) only compounded the uneasiness of farm families. Califano came to the job with the goal of making the nation smoke free, and under his watch, HEW inaugurated a series of federal anti-smoking campaigns. Growers saw this campaign as a betrayal of the government's support. Farmers called for Califano's job (and worse). The city council of South Boston, an important Virginia market town, went so far as to pass a resolution calling on Congress "to censure Secretary Califano for unjustly singling out one industry and to withhold from appropriations the funds cited by the Secretary for the use in his misguided program." The anger was so intense that President Carter had to travel to Wilson, North Carolina, by then home to the largest tobacco market in the United States, to reassure growers that his support for health research in no way indicated a lack of support for the Federal Tobacco Program. "As long as I am in the White House," he told farmers and buyers crowded along rows of tobacco ready to be auctioned, "we will have a good loan program for tobacco in the federal government."[10]

The anger about Califano's actions was just a symptom of a deeper unease that had set in among tobacco farmers. The president of the Danville Tobacco Association summed up the fears of many in 1979 when he noted that the combination of the fuss over allotment leasing and "a government . . . fighting the tobacco program on one hand and supporting it on the other, signal the end of the tobacco program as we know it." Therefore, he told members, use "everything in your power, both politically and monetarily to save the tobacco program."[11]

Sensing that the federal government was a shaky partner, an increasing number of growers sought what they considered to be their natural allies in the struggle to protect tobacco: the tobacco companies. Tobacco companies had, in fact, been cultivating growers to be their allies for some time in response to their own publicity problems.

In the years following World War II, studies emerged showing a definitive link between cigarette use and cancer. There had long been evidence that tobacco use was not healthy, of course, but these studies brought renewed attention to the health problems of tobacco users, especially cigarette smokers. A 1952 Reader's Digest article that compiled the results of a number of studies linking tobacco and disease prompted public panic. The following year, a study that found that 44 percent of mice exposed to cigarette smoke condensate developed tumors only fueled the fire. Neither of these reports had the impact of the Surgeon General's 1964 report Smoking and Health, which officially linked smoking to numerous health problems for the first time. This report initiated what had been a 40-year struggle to make tobacco control a public health priority.[12]

Manufacturers did their best to dodge the issue. In the wake of early reports, they attempted to allay public fears by adding filters to their cigarettes and making other cosmetic changes to downplay the risks of smoking. However, they soon found it better to respond by alternately ignoring and denying the results of the various studies. Attacking the methods of studies that linked cigarettes to disease, they grabbed at statistical straws to argue that no study had conclusively linked smoking and disease and hired respected scientists, such as the former head of the National Cancer Institute, to downplay the risks. All the while, they buried the findings of their own researchers that corroborated the findings of outside researchers.[13]

To publicize their side of the tobacco debates, manufacturers created powerful lobbying and public relations organizations. In 1953, they formed the Tobacco Industry Research Council (TIRC) to combat studies that linked tobacco and disease; the council's main strategy was coordinated media assaults on such research. In 1958, they created the Tobacco Institute to be the industry's voice in both the public and political arenas. Defining anti-tobacco forces broadly—from researchers who were investigating the health risks of tobacco use to legislators who were seeking increases in tobacco taxes to local leaders who were pushing for even modest smoking bans—the Tobacco Institute used denial, deceit, and, most importantly, deep pockets to press the industry's cause. Until it was disbanded in 1998 as part of the multistate tobacco settlement, the Tobacco Institute was one of the most powerful industry trade groups in the nation.[14]

Increasing external pressure led growers and manufacturers to rally around one another. The Tobacco Institute and Tobacco Associates, Inc., a trade group for promoting flue-cured tobacco exports, bankrolled the Tobacco Growers' Information Committee (TGIC), which was designed to serve as both the growers' voice and a clearinghouse to provide growers with information about tobacco taxes, medical findings, and "other . . . existing or proposed punitive or discriminatory legislation . . . against tobacco or tobacco products." Membership in the TGIC was open only to "national, regional, state or local organizations" with an interest in the tobacco trade, including growers' groups and warehousemen's associations. Its first executive committee was a sort of who's-who of tobacco state notables, including Stabilization president Carl T. Hicks, who served as the TGIC's first chairman.[15]

The important role Stabilization and numerous other growers' organizations—especially Farm Bureaus in tobacco states—took in the TGIC allowed it to claim that it spoke for growers, but it would be misleading to characterize the TGIC as a growers' organization. Despite the Tobacco Institute's claim that the TGIC was "a grass-roots type of organization," it might be better described as a corporate vehicle for rallying growers. Nearly all of the TGIC's funding came from the Tobacco Institute and Tobacco Associates, Inc., and while it is unclear how much control these organizations exerted over the day-to-day operation of the TGIC, their fingerprints were all over its handiwork. TGIC newsletters and press releases relied heavily on Tobacco Institute sources. Quotes from TGIC officials regularly appeared in Tobacco Institute press releases, and officers from each organization spoke regularly at the others' meetings. This is not to say that the TGIC was simply a front for tobacco manufacturers—the committee clearly represented a broad constituency with a common interest in preserving the tobacco economy—but financial support for the organization was a product of manufacturers' understanding that growers made a much more sympathetic public face than large corporations.[16]

Debates about tobacco expanded beyond public health to include the economic and cultural ramifications of tobacco control on the lives of thousands of farm families. In the late 1970s, the Tobacco Institute released a series of advertisements that highlighted the economic impact of tobacco on rural areas. One such ad depicted a lush tobacco field that it described as "Tobaccoland, U.S.A." Under a headline declaring, "This Good Green American Land Does a Lot More than Just Grow Tobacco," the ad pleaded the case of tobacco farmers by pointing to the crop's long history in America and the estimated 500,000 farm families involved in its production. Similarly, R. J. Reynolds's "Pride in Tobacco" campaign, which began in 1978, distributed tens of thousands of hats and T-shirts and more than 200,000 bumper stickers with a picture of hand filled with tobacco leaves giving a "thumbs up" to farm families. All of these media campaigns were designed to present the wholesome image of beleaguered growers as a face for the industry.[17]

It was actually more of a mask, and it could hide only so much of the strained relationship between farm families and manufacturers. Growers continued to complain of low prices and bad faith. One young Virginia farmer complained when the "substantially higher prices" tobacco companies promised in 1975 failed to materialize. "I believed in the wisdom of the tobacco companies . . . and planted more tobacco," he said, expressing his feelings of betrayal when they offered excuses when prices ended up being lower than the prior year. "There must be better answers than these to the many questions that haunt the tobacco farmers . . . that are being put out of business." In his frustration, North Carolina farmer Henry Farrell penned a bit of verse that depicted farmers playing in a yearlong craps game in which manufacturers have loaded the dice. Every season brings a new gamble for the farmer, but not for the "men in tailored suits." At season's end, the dice are hurled:

The farmer draws back his fist. It's raining, the weather seems fine.
He flings the dice in a blur of spots. Farmers luck—they turn up nine.
The odds are high. The leafmen raise the pot some more.
Then neath a gambler's oath the dice tumble cross the auction floor.

Somewhere outside the sun is shining.
Somewhere there's a birddog whining.
Somewhere you can hear the school kids shout.
Down on that damn, dusty warehouse floor,
A tobacco farmer just crapped out.

His meter may have been suspect, but not his feel for the mood on Tobacco Road.[18]

The Republican takeover of the Senate in 1981 gave more power to tobacco manufacturers in the debates over the Federal Tobacco Program. Senator Jesse Helms of North Carolina rose to the chairmanship of the Senate Agriculture, Forestry and Nutrition Committee. Since his election in 1970 as a Republican, Helms had become the standard-bearer for the tobacco companies, especially R. J. Reynolds. His ascension gave anti-smoking advocates and liberals an opportunity to attack their common enemy. Hoping to embarrass Helms, they pushed for elimination of the tobacco program in the 1981 farm bill. Helms and his tobacco-state allies blocked the amendment, but its popularity among average Americans forced them to agree to revamp the program to limit government expenditures on tobacco. In 1982, they agreed to the creation of the No Net Cost program, which required farmers to pay an assessment for each pound of tobacco marketed into a fund designated to pay back Stabilization's outstanding loans to the CCC. In addition, the No Net Cost legislation implemented a number of reforms aimed at getting allotments back into the hands of actual growers. The corrections proved ineffective; Stabilization continued to find itself storing more tobacco it could not sell, and the increasingly hard times led more allotment owners to give up farming and lease their allotments.[19]

The failure of No Net Cost not only deepened the battle lines between tobacco and anti-tobacco forces, it also spurred a legislative civil war within the so-called tobacco family that raged for another decade. On one side stood Representative Charlie Rose, a moderate Democrat and longtime supporter of the program; on the other was Helms. Their first showdown came in 1983, when Rose offered a comprehensive solution to the Federal Tobacco Program's woes. In exchange for reductions in both parity prices and the No Net Cost assessments growers paid, the government would raise the federal tobacco tax. In Rose's calculation, the deal would have made American-grown leaf more desirable on the global market while shifting the costs of the Federal Tobacco Program from farm families to tobacco companies (and, ultimately, to smokers). Helms killed Rose's bill in committee, arguing that its tax increase would harm the tobacco industry.[20]

Helms and Rose continued to spar over the best way to support the nation's tobacco economy for the next two years as Stabilization's situation grew worse and farm families faced higher and higher assessments under the No Net Cost program. Every proposal Rose made that was intended to stabilize the Federal Tobacco Program by shifting the costs of the program to buyers met defeat by Helms's hand. Helms, meanwhile, tried to cast Rose as something of a fifth columnist for anti-tobacco forces. In 1985, Helms introduced his own bill, but it involved little more than an agreement that the Treasury Department would forgive Stabilization's debt; in exchange, tobacco companies would buy its excess tobacco at a deep discount. It included no provisions for improving the lot of small farm families; in fact, it included reductions in price supports. Despite this, farmers, fearful that antismoking legislators might axe the program altogether, threw their support behind Helms. The bill passed, but predictably, it did not fix the program's problems.[21]

By the 1990s, tobacco farm families and others in the industry had to admit that the Federal Tobacco Program was not sustainable. Even as they benefited from price supports, growers recognized that the inflated prices their crops sold for made it difficult for them to compete on the world market against foreign growers, especially those in China and Brazil, whose tobacco production had been increasing both in real terms and in relation to U.S. production since the 1960s. At the same time, declining U.S. consumption also made it clear to growers that relying on domestic markets alone could not save them. Allotment reductions to accommodate declining demand only emphasized that point.

Larger growers frustrated by the costs of leasing allotments began pushing for an end to the program. But one problem confronted them: what to do with the thousands of small growers who depended on federal supports and others across the region who earned income from leasing their allotments? Economists predicted devastation for these people and their local economies if the program was simply eliminated. Given the potential for harm, no politician dared suggest that the program be done away with overnight.

Eliminating the Federal Tobacco Program became contingent on politicians finding a way to compensate farmers for the losses they would suffer. The idea did not catch on immediately. Many anti-tobacco activists balked at the very idea, and even many small growers were cool to it. In 1994, the North Carolina Grange rejected a buyout proposal by Representative Charlie Rose. It was not until 1997, when Senator Richard Lugar introduced a $15 billion buyout plan that the issue took on any urgency. Lugar's plan was ultimately obviated by legislation providing tobacco growers with transition funds out of a larger federal settlement with tobacco manufacturers. The idea of a buyout did not go away, and it became clear that stopgap solutions could not address the hardships smaller growers faced or the global competitive disadvantage larger growers faced. In the early 2000s, new legislation calling for a buyout finally came up for vigorous debate in Congress. This time growers, industry leaders, and tobacco-state politicians supported it. When anti-smoking advocates came on board, enough momentum was finally found to pass the bill in 2004. The Federal Tobacco Program was finally dead, at the hands of its longtime friends.[22]

The auction houses went down with it. In fact, they began dying off even before the buyout. In 2000 alone, fifteen North Carolina warehouses shut their doors; by 2002, there was only one warehouse left in Forsyth County, where dozens of burgeoning warehouses had once stood in the shadow of R. J. Reynolds's massive Winston-Salem factory. Tobacco manufacturers hoping to streamline their supply lines instead contracted with growers who were searching for some price guarantees in an era of declining allotments. By 2001, an estimated 80 percent of the flue-cured crop bypassed the auction houses and went directly to manufacturers. "I'm afraid the auctions are about gone, like the dinosaur," one longtime auctioneer lamented. "I thought the auction system was a good system. It worked for a hundred years." His fears were soon confirmed. With the end of the Federal Tobacco

Program, all growers began making contracts directly with tobacco companies to guarantee that they would have a market for their crops at the end of the year.[23]

Fall still brings a rush and bustle in the Old Bright Belt as the few remaining tobacco farmers rush to ready the crops for sale. Only now there is no auction to anticipate, just a trip to the tobacco company's receiving center to drop off their loads. The only gamble they face now is if their tobacco is good enough to get them another contract for the next year.

Conclusion

A Dead End for Tobacco Road?

A trip through the Old Bright Belt today might lead one to wonder why it was ever called that. In the region's urban and suburban areas, allusions to bright tobacco in the names of subdivisions are about all that remain to remind residents of an agricultural past. There are still some farms in the rural parts, but, as expected, the buyout pushed out all but the largest growers. Three years after the buyout, the already-reduced number of farms fell even more; region-wide in 2007, there was roughly one-third the number of farms there had been in 2002. Henry County, Virginia, had two farms left. The 2012 census will no doubt show a further decline in the number of farms.[1]

The elimination of price controls and the rise of direct contracting have proven to be a boon for the larger growers. At lower prices, American tobacco sells well and the large growers have been able to make up the difference in volume, as they had hoped. The fact that growers still produce two-thirds of the tobacco in 2007 that was produced in 2002 reveals that those who expressed a desire to get bigger were not kidding. Some used their buyout money to invest in new tools that made more efficient production possible. Per farm production increased by 66 percent in that five-year period.

The post-buyout tobacco economy has presented some cruel ironies, though. While growers sought to become more independent, less constrained by government regulations, they have found themselves increasingly at the mercy of tobacco companies. Tobacco companies carefully monitor how the farmers who contract with them handle their fields and crops. They dictate, in fact, how growers are to cultivate and cure their crops. Any deviation could mean a lost contract, which most likely would mean the end of the farm. In this environment, growers manage much but really have little final say over their fields.[2]

The only thing they control, it seems, are the laborers, whose presence is the greatest sign of the changing times. Tobacco workers offer a far different scene in the fields and around the barns than the workers of earlier generations did. Most are men; tobacco work no longer follows the gendered division of labor that marked that of families. Rather than being seen as neighbors, they are a marginalized population, often living in mobile homes set apart from the houses of the locals, unseen by the communities in which they live.[3]

The realities of modern tobacco farm labor hardly resemble the world so many who grew up on tobacco farms in the twentieth century would remember. The family farms as they knew them have disappeared, replaced by new forms of plantations supplied by movable labor. Understandably, many have come to long for the so-called good old days of bright tobacco's supposed golden era. Books of memories and photographs have become something of a cottage industry, in fact. It is important not to idealize that world. It was far from perfect. However, it was a unique time in the history of southern agriculture. Its passing is sad, if only because of what's coming next.

Notes

Introduction

1. Killebrew and Myrick, *Tobacco Leaf*, 251–55; William Hawthorne interview with the author. For scientific information on the Carolina sphinx moth (*Manduca sexta*), see "Tobacco Hornworm," Featured Creatures Web site of the University of Florida Entomology and Nematology Department, http://entomology.ifas.ufl.edu/creatures/field /hornworm.htm, accessed 29 December 2013.

2. Smyth, *A Tour in the United States of America*, 2:132; Leftwich manuscript, Leftwich-Shepherd Bowles Family Papers, Library of Virginia; "Mr. and Mrs. Smithers Life History," 23 May 1939, WPA Life Histories Online, Collection, Library of Virginia, http:// image.lva.virginia.gov/WPL/00259, accessed 8 February 2014.

3. Meg Medina, "The Farm," *Style Weekly*, 6 November 2001, 19, 21.

4. Emmy Wilson and Claude W. Anderson, "Interview with Nancy Williams," in *Weevils in the Wheat: Interviews with Virginia Ex-Slaves*, edited by Charles L. Perdue Jr., Thomas E. Barden, and Robert K. Phillips (Charlottesville: University Press of Virginia, 1976), 322. Further testimony of the practice in antebellum Virginia is found in "On the Tobacco Plantation," *Scribner's Monthly* (October 1872): 653.

5. Orrell, *From the Seed to the Hand*, 1; Bennett, "Dubious Heritage"; "Oldtime Leaf Farming Is Focus," *Durham Herald-Sun*, 1 September 2008.

6. Tobacco is a highly adaptable plant and a number of varieties are grown in the U.S. South. Each is distinguished by how it is grown and cured and/or how it is used. There is some overlap in where varieties are grown, but most varieties have distinctive historical growing regions. Bright tobacco has the largest growing area, stretching from Virginia to South Carolina and in pockets of Georgia and Florida. Abutting the bright tobacco belt to the north is the quickly disappearing dark tobacco belt, which covers portions of Virginia and Maryland. Often called fire-cured tobacco, dark tobacco is a heat-cured variety from which bright tobacco was adapted. It is used primarily in pipe tobaccos, but cigarette manufacturers buy some of the crop. Burley tobacco is one of the two major U.S. tobacco varieties (the other is bright tobacco). It is an air-cured variety that is grown

primarily in Kentucky but also in Tennessee, western Virginia, and western North Carolina. Burley tobacco is very popular for its amenability to added flavor, making it very versatile. Its primary use is in chewing tobacco and other smokeless tobacco products, but cigarette manufacturers also use a great deal of the crop. Other varieties of tobacco are grown regionally in the United States—Connecticut farmers grow a shade-grown variety used for cigar manufacturing, for example—but no region matches the South in the extent of tobacco grown. For a recent history of the origins of bright tobacco, see Hahn, *Making Tobacco Bright*.

7. For the political power of the sugar industry, see Hahamovitch, *No Man's Land*; and Hollander, *Raising Cane in the 'Glades*. For chicken raising, see Striffler, *Chicken*.

Chapter 1. Family

1. "Resume of the Attached Preliminary Report on the Cost of Virginia Dark Fired-Cured and Bright Tobacco for 1922," Box 1028, General Correspondence of the Office of the Secretary of Agriculture, Records of the Office of the Secretary of Agriculture, Record Group (hereafter RG) 16, National Archives and Records Administration (hereafter NARA). Census figures confirm the assertion in this report. In 1919, four out of five Charlotte County farmers reported hiring no workers, and those who did paid out an average of $211 for the year, far below what the researchers believed would be necessary. All census calculations in this chapter compiled from Historical Census Browser, University of Virginia, Geospatial and Statistical Data Center, http://mapserver.lib.virginia.edu.

2. "Narrative Report of the County Agent, 1926: Bedford County, Virginia," Extension Service Annual Narrative and Statistical Reports, Virginia, Reel 19, RG 33.6, NARA; "Annual Report of the Home Demonstration Work for Women and Girls, 1920: Brunswick County, Va.," Extension Service Annual Narrative and Statistical Reports, Virginia, Reel 5, RG 33.6, NARA; Vernon and Ezekiel, *Causes of Profit or Loss on Virginia Tobacco Farms*, 18.

3. Somers, *The Southern States since the War*, 21.

4. Kerr-Ritchie, *Freedpeople in the Tobacco South*, 130–38.

5. "Tobacco versus Wheat and Corn," *Southern Planter and Farmer*, May 1868, 2; "The True Condition of Southside Virginia, and Her Only Remedy," *Southern Planter and Farmer*, December 1875, 12; Kerr-Ritchie, *Freedpeople in the Tobacco South*, 97; Scharrer, *A Kind of Fate*, 62–65.

6. C. D. Whittle to "My Beloved Boy," Lewis Neale Whittle Papers, Southern Historical Collection, quoted in Roark, *Masters without Slaves*, 155; Langhorne, *Southern Sketches from Virginia*, 37; "White vs. Negro Labor," *Southern Planter and Farmer*, January 1868, 43.

7. "Contract between Two Virginia Farmers and Two Virginia Freedmen," in Hahn et al., *Freedom*, 737–38.

8. Ibid.; "Goodwyn Agricultural Club: Essay upon the Subject of Labor," *Southern Planter and Farmer*, March 1871, 135; "Evening Session," *Southern Planter and Farmer*, February 1867, 40.

9. Contract between G. C. Hannah and several freedpeople, December 1865, Hannah Family Papers, Section 41, Virginia Historical Society (hereafter VHS); Robert L. Ragland, "Farm Labor," in Southern Fertilizing Company, *Tobacco: The Outlook for 1875,* 27, 30. "Old Josh Dover" [Ed Currin], 12, Federal Writers' Project Papers, Folder 310, Southern Historical Collection, University of North Carolina, Chapel Hill (hereafter SHC); *Farmer and Mechanic* (Raleigh, N.C.), 1 April 1880, 1.

10. "Commander of the Military District of Lynchburg to the Freedmen's Bureau Commissioner, Enclosing Seven Orders by the District Commander," in Hahn et al., *Freedom,* 249; Capt. Hugo Hildebrandt to Justice of the Peace of Caswell County, 3 October 1867, Records of Field Offices, North Carolina, Reel 18, Records of the Bureau of Refugees, Freedmen, and Abandoned Lands, RG 105, NARA; "Evening Session," *Southern Planter and Farmer,* February 1867, 40; Hunter, *Useful Information Concerning Yellow Tobacco,* 13.

11. "Freedmen's Bureau Assistant Superintendent at Amelia Court House, Virginia, to the Freedmen's Bureau Superintendent of the 2nd District of Virginia, Enclosing a Circular by the Assistant Superintendent," in Hahn et al., *Freedom,* 985–88.

12. "Large Negro Departure from Virginia," Reprinted in the *New York Times,* 23 January 1870.

13. *Columbus Daily Enquirer,* 5 October 1866; "North Carolina Freedmen's Bureau Assistant Commissioner to the Freedmen's Bureau Commissioner," in Hahn et al., *Freedom,* 963.

14. Trelease, *White Terror,* 195–96, 211; *Hearings before the United States Senate Select Committee to Investigate Alleged Outrages in Southern States: Testimony on North Carolina, with Minority Report,* 145, 372.

15. *Hearings before the United States Senate Select Committee to Investigate Alleged Outrages in Southern States: Testimony on North Carolina, with Minority Report,* 346.

16. Woodman, *New South—New Law,* 60, 51–54. See also Kerr-Ritchie, *Freedpeople in the Tobacco South,* 160–63.

17. "Southside Virginia," *Southern Planter,* July 1883, 320; Censer, *The Reconstruction of White Southern Womanhood,* 139; "Enquiries," *Southern Planter,* June 1883, 286; Armistead Burwell to Edward Bouldin Burwell, 8 December 1887 and 20 October 1891, Burwell Family Papers, Section 9, VHS.

18. Censer, *The Reconstruction of White Southern Womanhood,* 128–45; Bolton, *Poor Whites of the Antebellum South,* 27–33.

19. Hagood, *Mothers of the South,* 81–82.

20. Landon, "The Tobacco Growing Industry in North Carolina," 251; Rental Contract, Samuel C. Hubbard, Box 1, Folder 1, and James H. Guthrie to Samuel C. Hubbard, 7 July 1891, Box 1, Folder 4, Samuel C. Hubbard Papers, David M. Rubenstein Rare Book and Manuscript Library, Duke University.

21. Response to Sidney Frissell survey by S. R. Blair, 28 February 1928, Folder 95, Box 7, Tobacco Growers' Cooperative Association Papers, SHC.

22. Banks, "Tobacco Talk," 40–41.

23. Holt, *Making Freedom Pay*, 93–99; Sampson White to E. Dana Durand, September 1910, reprinted in Kerr-Ritchie, *Freedpeople in the Tobacco South*, 255.

24. "Tobacco Bag Stringing Operations in North Carolina and Virginia," 1939, North Carolina Collection, http://www.lib.unc.edu/ncc/tbs/tbs084.html.

25. Allen Tullos, Oral History Interview with Betty and Lloyd Davidson, 2 and 15 February 1979, Interview H-19, Southern Oral History Program Collection, SHC, http://docsouth.unc.edu/nc/davidson/davidson.html.

26. Shirley, *From Congregation Town to Industrial City*, 194; Janiewski, *Sisterhood Denied*, 56. Farmers in the Piedmont were not the only ones to combine farm and off-farm work; this was a common strategy across the rural South by the early twentieth century. See Newby, *Plain Folk in the New South*, 61–62.

27. Jones, "Bank Loans in North Carolina in 1915," 49–57; Landon, "The Tobacco Growing Industry in North Carolina," 252; Harris, *The Negro as Capitalist*, 191–92; "Report of the County Agent, 1919: Mecklenburg County, Virginia," Extension Service Annual Narrative and Statistical Reports, Virginia, Reel 4, RG 33.6, NARA.

28. Bennett, "Of the Quest of the Golden Leaf," 201.

29. Perman, *The Road to Redemption*, 238–39; U.S. Department of Agriculture, *Report of the Commissioner of Agriculture for 1867*, 104; Address by Col. William H. Burgwyn, *The Gold Leaf* (Henderson, N.C.), 3 November 1887; "Henderson's Romantic Wedding—Sale of Oxford County Farms—The Bright Tobacco Region," Richmond *Times*, March 8, 1895, 2; Killebrew, *Report on the Culture and Curing of Tobacco in the United States*, 121; Armistead Burwell to Edward Bouldin Burwell, 20 October 1891, Burwell Family Papers, Section 9, VHS.

30. Schweninger, *Black Property Owners in the South*, 173. In 1920, there were seventy-five black landowners and sixty-nine white landowners in Burwell's neighborhood. Most were farmers, but some earned money at other pursuits, including as washerwomen and farm laborers. Compiled from federal manuscript census, 1920, District 52, Clarksville, Mecklenburg County, Virginia, Ancestry.com, accessed 8 February 2014. These figures omit individuals enumerated in the town limits of Clarksville.

31. Rawick, *The American Slave*, 220. I have taken the liberty of removing the dialect the interviewer used in recording the interview but have not changed any words.

32. Bennett, "Of the Quest of the Golden Leaf," 186. For African Americans' strategies for landownership, see Holt, *Making Freedom Pay*, 52–99; and Kerr-Ritchie, *Freedpeople in the Tobacco South*, 209–45.

33. Untitled article, *The Crisis*, 10, no. 1 (May 1915): 21.

34. U.S. Senate, *Report of the Committee of the Senate upon the Relations between Labor and Capital*, 4:7

35. Rawick, *The American Slave*, 289–90.

36. North Carolina Department of Labor and Printing, *Thirtieth Annual Report of the Department of Labor and Printing of the State of State of North Carolina*, 18–20; U.S. Department of Commerce, Bureau of the Census, *Fourteenth Census of the United States*.

State Compendium: Virginia and *Fourteenth Census of the United States. State Compendium: North Carolina*, Agriculture, Tables 1 and 4. It is difficult to know if statistics for 1919 are representative of other years because of the situation during World War I. Tobacco prices were high, so many growers put in additional acres, often leading to increases in demand for labor, but the wartime labor situation, especially the development of the Great Migration, meant that laborers were often difficult to secure.

Chapter 2. Hands

1. Interview with Walter Corbett, 2 December 1938, Folder 282, Federal Writers' Project Papers, SHC; Barefoot and Kornegay, *Mules and Memories*, 36; Hagood, *Mothers of the South*, 89.

2. "Report of the County Agent, 1921: Vance County, N.C.," Reel 12, Extension Service Annual Narrative and Statistical Reports, RG 33.6, NARA.

3. Berry, "Our Tobacco Problem," 17–18; Yeargin, *Remembering North Carolina Tobacco*, 14.

4. "Narrative Report of the County Agent, 1930: Halifax County, Va.," Reel 30, Extension Service Annual Narrative and Statistical Reports, RG 33.6, NARA; Killebrew, *Report on the Culture and Curing of Tobacco in the United States*, 117.

5. Stockard, "Daughter of the Piedmont," manuscript, SHC; Ledger, 1922–23, Miller Family Papers, VHS.

6. Hahn, *Making Tobacco Bright*, 107, 122; Ledger, 1922–23, Miller Family Papers, VHS.

7. "Mr. and Mrs. Smithers Life History," WPA Life History Collection, Library of Virginia; Johnson, "Life on a North Carolina Tobacco Farm in the 1920's," 13, North Carolina Collection; "Daughter of the Piedmont"; Rice and Payne, *The Seventeenth Child*, 48–49; Sallie Walker Stockard, "Daughter of the Piedmont," manuscript, SHC, University of North Carolina, Chapel Hill.

8. Ragland, *Tobacco, from the Seed to the Salesroom*, 14.

9. J. W. Leftwich, "Prize Essay on the Culture, Curing, and Subsequent Management of Fine Yellow Tobacco," *Southern Planter and Farmer*, August 1870, 2.

10. Rice and Payne, *The Seventeenth Child*, 50; Betty Jackson, "Good Things and Nasty Things on the Farm," in Lasley and Holt, *A Prayer for the Baby Goat*, 42.

11. H. G. Jones, interview with the author; Rice and Payne, *The Seventeenth Child*, 50.

12. "Narrative Report of the County Agent, 1925: Vance County, N.C.," Reel 26, Extension Service Annual Narrative and Statistical Reports, RG 33.6, NARA; U.S. Department of Agriculture, *Tobacco Culture*, 18–21; W. Kerr Scott (County Agent) to Alamance County Farmers, in "Narrative Report of the County Agent, 1926: Alamance County, N.C.," Reel 27, Extension Service Annual Narrative and Statistical Reports, RG 33.6, NARA; American Tobacco Company, "The Story of the Fight Against Blue Mold" in *Producing Finer Flue Cured Tobacco*, Box 2, Folder 23, John H. Hager Papers, VHS.

13. Bradsher, "Tobacco Culture and Manufacture in North Carolina, part 1," 297;

Johnson, "Life on a North Carolina Tobacco Farm in the 1920's," 15–16, North Carolina Collection.

14. Hagood, *Mothers of the South*, 86.

15. Federal Writers' Project of North Carolina, "Gamblers All," 108–9, Charles Horace Hamilton Papers, SCRC.

16. Spirn, *Daring to Look*, 100.

17. Hagood, *Mothers of the South*, 87.

18. William Hawthorne, interview with the author; "Report of the County Agent, 1945: Durham County, N.C.," Box 223, Extension Service Annual Narrative and Statistical Reports, RG 33.6, NARA; "Narrative Report of the County Agent, 1943: Vance County, N.C.," Reel 136, Extension Service Annual Narrative and Statistical Reports, RG 33.6, NARA.

19. Betty McGlawhorn, "The Good Life," in Yeargin, *Remembering North Carolina Tobacco*, 108–9.

20. Johnson, "Life on a North Carolina Tobacco Farm in the 1920's," 15–16, North Carolina Collection; McGlawhorn, "The Good Life," 109–10; Lasley and Holt, *A Prayer for the Baby Goat*, 46.

21. Bruce Woodard, "Tobacco Cultivation," in Yeargin, *Remembering North Carolina Tobacco*, 29.

22. *Yadkin Valley News*, 2 October 1891.

23. "Daughter of the Piedmont"; John H. Abner, interview by Walter Corbett, 2 December 1938, Folder 282, Federal Writers' Project Papers, SHC; William Hawthorne, interview with the author; Lasley and Holt, *A Prayer for the Baby Goat*, 57.

24. Tennis, *Beach to Bluegrass*, 46–47; Garner, *North Carolina Barbecue*, 22–23; H. G. Jones to Shelby Stephenson, 1 May 2002, in author's possession; Federal Writers' Project of North Carolina, "Gamblers All," 109, Charles Horace Hamilton Papers, SCRC; interview with Salina McMillon, 25 October 1976, Interview H-0208, Southern Oral History Program Collection, SHC.

25. Hagood, *Mothers of the South*, 88; Phillips, "Farm Women of Stokes County, North Carolina," 134.

26. Hagood, *Mothers of the South*, 90.

27. Bennett, "Dubious Heritage," 23–40.

28. "Report of the County Agent, 1919: Person County, N.C.," Reel 8, Extension Service Annual Narrative and Statistical Reports, RG 33.6, NARA; interview with Walter Corbett, 2 December 1938, Folder 282, Federal Writers' Project Papers, SHC.

Chapter 3. Tobacco-Raising Fools

Epigraph source: Earl Booth (Concord Depot, Va.), letter to the editor of *Tri-State Tobacco Grower*, April 1924.

1. *The Gold Leaf* (Henderson, N.C.), 21 February 1884, 1.

2. "Narrative Report of the County Agent, 1931: Stokes County, N.C.," Reel 52, Extension Service Annual Narrative and Statistical Reports, RG 33.6, NARA.

3. For the history of the loose-leaf auction method and its importance to bright tobacco, see Tilley, *The Bright-Tobacco Industry*, 197–250; and Hahn, *Making Tobacco Bright*, 110–12.

4. "Narrative Report of the County Agent (Negro), 1942: Guilford County, N.C.," Reel 125, Extension Service Annual Narrative and Statistical Reports, North Carolina, RG 33.6, NARA.

5. Bradsher, "Tobacco Culture and Manufacture in North Carolina, part 2," 380; Killebrew and Myrick, *Tobacco Leaf*, 279–80; Leighton, *Southern Harvest*, 132; Fitzpatrick, "Language of the Tobacco Market," 132.

6. *Men, Places and Things as Noted by Benjamin Simpson* (Danville, Va.: Dance Bros, 1891), quoted in Tilley, "Agitation against the American Tobacco Company in North Carolina, 1890–1911," 210–11.

7. Woofter, *The Plight of Cigarette Tobacco*, 42.

8. Hagood, *Mothers of the South*, 77.

9. "New Orders Boost Tobacco Prices," *South Hill Enterprise*, 7 November 1929; T. E. Winston, letter to the editor, *Tri-State Tobacco Grower*, January 1923.

10. Hagood, *Mothers of the South*, 16.

11. Phillips, "Farm Women of Stokes County," 69; interview with Salina McMillon, 25 October 1976, Interview H-0208, Southern Oral History Program Collection, SHC; Barefoot and Kornegay, *Mules and Memories*, 102.

12. Woofter, *The Plight of Cigarette Tobacco*, 42; F. Beverly, "How She Gained the Coop. Spirit," *Tri-State Tobacco Grower*, October 1923; *Progressive Farmer*, 9 April 1889, quoted in Tilley, *The Bright-Tobacco Industry*, 405.

13. W. T. Sutherlin, "Tobacco Culture," *The Gold Leaf* (Henderson, N.C.), 27 January 1887; *The Gold Leaf*, 23 February 1888; *Yadkin Valley News* (Mount Airy, N.C.), 28 May 1887; *The Gold Leaf*, 23 December 1886.

14. *The Gold Leaf*, 17 March 1887; Bruce, *The Plantation Negro as a Freeman*, 182–83; "The Labor Difficulty in the South," *Southern Planter*, June 1905, 475; Flannagan, "Virginia Tobacco," 5.

15. *Yadkin Valley News*, (Mount Airy, N.C.) 20 November 1891; John E. Hughes, President's Report, 12 June 1916, Records of the Danville Tobacco Association, Library of Virginia.

16. *The Gold Leaf* (Henderson, N.C.), 8 November 1888; *Yadkin Valley News* (Mount Airy, N.C.), 13 November 1891.

17. Advertisement, *The Gold Leaf*, 14 February 1889; J. E. Bennett to Thomas Carroll, 29 September 1886, Thomas Carroll Papers, David M. Rubenstein Rare Book and Manuscript Library, Duke University.

18. Woofter, *The Plight of Cigarette Tobacco*, 43.

19. Danville Tobacco Association to Tobacco Buyers, 1927, Danville, Va., Records of

the Danville Tobacco Association, Library of Virginia; Woofter, *The Plight of Cigarette Tobacco*, 48.

20. Charles E. Fuller, letter to the editor of *The Carolina Union Farmer*, 24 August 1911; Federal Writers' Project of North Carolina, "Gamblers All," 427, Charles Horace Hamilton Papers, SCRC; Woofter, *The Plight of Cigarette Tobacco*, 45, 48.

21. Banks, "Tobacco Talk," 41.

22. "Proper Assorting of Tobacco," *The Gold Leaf* (Henderson, N.C.), 8 November 1888.

23. President's Report, 12 June 1916, Records of the Danville Tobacco Association, Library of Virginia. For the evolution of the definition of bright tobacco, see Hahn, *Making Tobacco Bright*; Tilley, *The Bright-Tobacco Industry*, 319.

24. Buck, *The Granger Movement*, 58–59; Tilley, *The Bright-Tobacco Industry*, 397–405. For the history of the Grange in the South, see Saloutos, *Farmer Movements in the South, 1865–1933*, 31–44.

25. "Richmond Letter," *Bristol News*, 16 January 1877, 2; Tilley, *The Bright-Tobacco Industry*, 401–5.

26. "Virginia State Grange," *Southern Planter and Farmer*, March 1877, 190.

27. Robert L. Ragland, "Tobacco Inspections," *Southern Planter and Farmer*, March 1875, 152.

28. John J. Wilkinson, letter to the editor of *Southern Planter and Farmer*, August 1874, 107.

29. "Patrons of Husbandry," *Southern Planter and Farmer*, April 1874, 1; "Mr. St. Andrew and the Granger Movement," *Southern Planter and Farmer*, September 1874, 152.

30. "Patrons of Husbandry," *Southern Planter and Farmer*, April 1874, 1; National Grange, *Manual of the Subordinate Granges of the Patrons of Husbandry*, 9th ed., 104–6; D. Wyatt Aiken, "The Patrons of Husbandry," *Southern Planter and Farmer*, July 1872, 404; Marti, *Women of the Grange*, 23–27.

31. D. Wyatt Aiken, "The Patrons of Husbandry," *Southern Planter and Farmer*, July 1872, 404; "Patrons of Husbandry," *Southern Planter and Farmer*, April 1874, 1.

32. "Coalition Rule in Danville—The Danville Circular, 1883," italics in original. Funders tended to describe Readjuster leadership as "negro rule" even when the politicians were white. Danville's leading Funders had this circular published in newspapers around the state to convince white farmers, especially in western Virginia and the Shenandoah Valley, to side with the Democrats in the 1883 election. Inflating the perception of black rule as destructive, they hoped to convince farmers in areas with smaller black populations to drop their support for the Readjuster coalition. "After the Danville Riot," *New York Times*, 28 November 1883; U.S. Senate, Committee on Privileges and Elections, *Inquiry into Massacre of Colored Men at Danville, Va., and Alleged Election Outrages in Virginia, in 1883*, 1176, 1274–75. For the connection of tobacco inspection to the political scene, see Kerr-Ritchie, *Freedpeople in the Tobacco South*, 146–48.

33. For the Danville riot, see Dailey, *Before Jim Crow*, 103–31.

34. Garlock, *Guide to the Local Assemblies of the Knights of Labor*.

35. H. G. Ellis to T. V. Powderly, 17 August 1886; R. W. Kruse to T. V. Powderly, 3 August 1886; R. J. C. M. W., letter to the editor, *Journal of United Labor*, 11 June 1887, all in Foner and Lewis, *The Black Worker*, 255, 274.

36. The literature on the Farmers' Alliance and subsequent Populist movement is vast. For the most recent accounts of the national movement, see Postel, *The Populist Vision*; and Sanders, *Roots of Reform*, 117–47. For the movement in the South, see McMath, *Populist Vanguard*; and Ayers, *The Promise of the New South*, 214–82. The best modern accounts of the Farmers' Alliance and populism in Virginia and North Carolina are Steelman, *The North Carolina Farmers' Alliance*; Beeby, *Revolt of the Tar Heels*; Creech, *Righteous Indignation*; and Kerr-Ritchie, *Freedpeople in the Tobacco South*, 181–207.

37. McMath, *Populist Vanguard*, 38–40, quote on 39–40; Tilley, *The Bright-Tobacco Industry*, 406.

38. *The Gold Leaf* (Henderson, N.C.), 18 July 1889; John C. Clark to Elias Carr, 18 November 1889, Box 7, Folder 96, L. L. Polk Papers, SHC; A. M. Stock to Charles N. Vance, 14 August 1890, Box 7, Folder 104, Vance Papers, SHC; John Tipton to Zebulon Vance, 26 July 1890, Box 7, Folder 102, Zebulon Baird Vance Papers, SHC.

39. "Virginia State Alliance," *Southern Planter*, 1 October 1890.

40. Kerr-Ritchie, *Freedpeople in the Tobacco South*, 200.

41. For the history of the Colored Farmers' Alliance, see Ali, *In the Lion's Mouth*, 48–77.

42. Spriggs, "The Virginia Colored Farmers' Alliance," 199; Kerr-Ritchie, *Freedpeople in the Tobacco South*, 206. Many of these members were in the Norfolk area, but Virginia's southern Piedmont was the second-greatest area of concentration.

43. Ali, *In the Lion's Mouth*, 59–61; Kerr-Ritchie, *Freedpeople in the Tobacco South*, 205; Spriggs, "The Virginia Colored Farmers' Alliance," 197.

44. Ali, *In the Lion's Mouth*, 62–63, quote on 62.

45. Steelman, *The North Carolina Farmers' Alliance*, 19.

46. "A Word to Farmers as Well as Others," *The Gold Leaf*, 1 December 1887.

47. Ibid.

48. Tilley, *The Bright-Tobacco Industry*, 409–11. Reference to the Alliance warehouse in Henderson in entry for 27 March 1890, vol. 26, Box 2, William Wallace White Diaries, SHC.

49. Steelman, *The North Carolina Farmers' Alliance*, 25; W. M. Evans to Zebulon B. Vance, 10 August 1890, Box 7, Folder 105, Zebulon Baird Vance Papers, SHC; D. P. Meacham to Zebulon Vance, 28 March 1890, Box 6, Folder 91, Zebulon Baird Vance Papers, SHC.

50. A. J. Dalby to Leonidas L. Polk, 10 January 1890, Box 7, Folder 97, L. L. Polk Papers, SHC; *Yadkin Valley News* (Mt. Airy, N.C.), 26 February 1892.

51. Steelman, *The North Carolina Farmers' Alliance*, 266–67.

52. Tilley, *The Bright-Tobacco Industry*, 262–65.

53. "The Tobacco Trust," newspaper clipping, 4 January 1900, vol. 168, 764, Clipping File through 1975, North Carolina Collection; Tilley, *The Bright-Tobacco Industry*, 382–83; "Southern Tobacco Growers," *Southern Planter*, October 1906, 802.

54. J. Bryan Grimes, "Speech to the Tobacco Growers Association," ca. 1899, North Carolina Collection.

55. Hahn, *Making Tobacco Bright*, 136–44. For a claim that the Mutual Protective Association of Bright Tobacco Growers represented 10,000 farmers, see "Tobacco Men Meet," *The State* (Columbia, S.C.), 18 December 1904. For attendance at meetings, see "Tobacco Growers Together," *Charlotte Daily Observer*, 18 November 1903; "To Fight Tobacco Trust," *Charlotte Daily Observer*, 3 October 1906; "Farmers at Danville, Va.," *Charlotte Daily Observer*, 9 January 1907; "Farmers in Convention," *Charlotte Daily Observer*, 2 May 1907; "Tobacco Growers Meet," *Charlotte Daily Observer*, 10 August 1907; "To Fight Tobacco Trust," *Charlotte Daily Observer*, 3 October 1906.

56. "Gold Rather than Lawful Money," *Charlotte Daily Observer*, 14 January 1900. The average amount of tobacco sold annually at Danville between 1900 and 1909 (38,014,118 lbs.) was 12.3 percent lower than the average annual amount sold between 1890 and 1899 (43,354,386 lbs.), but the expansion in the number of available auction warehouse in different towns is a more likely explanation. Even during the boom times of World War I, when tobacco production expanded, the amount sold at Danville exceeded the 1900–1909 annual average only once, in 1918. President's Reports, Danville Tobacco Association, 1984, Reel 2, Records of the Danville Tobacco Association, Library of Virginia. In 1907, rumors swelled that the bright tobacco acreage in Virginia and North Carolina had been cut drastically as a result of farmers organizing to limit their crops, but sales at Danville were down only 1.3 percent that year; "Bright Tobacco Shortage," *Wall Street Journal*, 1 August 1907.

57. The Black Patch war has been well documented by a number of historians. The most recent accounts are Marshall, *Violence in the Black Patch of Kentucky and Tennessee*; and Waldrep, *Night Riders*. In *The Politics of Despair*, Tracy Campbell compares the Black Patch war to the attempt of farmers in central Kentucky's Burley Belt to go on strike and withhold their crops from the ATC at the same time. Barbara Hahn compares the Black Patch war to the experience of farmers in the bright tobacco regions in *Making Tobacco Bright*, 147–57. See also "Night Riders Threat?," *Richmond Times Dispatch*, 30 September 1908; "Night Riders in Virginia," *Charlotte Daily Observer*, 21 March 1908; "Night Riders in This State," *Charlotte Daily Observer*, 4 May 1908; "Tobacco Barns Posted," *Charlotte Daily Observer*, 5 October 1908.

58. "Southern Tobacco Growers," *Southern Planter*, October 1906, 802; President's Report, 2 August 1908, 5–6, Records of the Danville Tobacco Association, Library of Virginia.

59. T. B. Parker, "Address to the North Carolina Tobacco Growers Association," ca. 1900, North Carolina Collection.

60. Saloutos, *Farmer Movements in the South*, 184; Barrett, *The Mission, History and Times of the Farmers' Union*, 25; Loomis, "The Rise and Decline of the North Carolina Farmers' Union," 312–14; U.S. House of Representatives, *Hearings before the Joint Commission to Investigate the Purchase of American-Grown Tobacco*, 3–4.

61. "Pool of Tobacco Ordered by Union," *Richmond Times Dispatch*, 18 August 1911.

62. Federal Writers' Project of North Carolina, "Gamblers All," 129, Charles Horace Hamilton Papers, SCRC.

63. Article 1, Section 14, in National Farmers' Union, *Constitution and By-Laws of the Farmers Educational and Co-Operative Union of America, Virginia Division*, 8; U.S. House of Representatives, *Hearings before the Joint Commission to Investigate the Purchase of American-Grown Tobacco*, 6, 24–25.

Chapter 4. Cooperation

1. *Southern Tobacco Journal*, 11 September 1917, quoted in Tilley, *The Bright-Tobacco Industry*, 389. Sales on the market floors of Danville, Virginia, the premier market in the northernmost bright tobacco–growing area known as the Old Bright Belt, are indicative of the increasing prices. In the period 1900–1914, prices averaged just over 11 cents per pound. From 1917 to 1919, the average price rose to nearly 41 cents per pound; Annual Market Statistics, Danville, Va., President's Report, 1984, Reel 2, Records of the Danville Tobacco Association, Library of Virginia; Report of Ned D. Morse, black demonstration agent, Mecklenburg County, Va., 1917, Extension Service Annual Narrative and Statistical Reports, Virginia, Reel 3, RG 33.6, NARA; Tilley, "Agitation against the American Tobacco Company in North Carolina, 1890–1911," 207–23; Report of the County Agent, 1919, Mecklenburg County, Virginia, Extension Service Annual Narrative and Statistical Reports, Virginia, RG 33.6, NARA.

2. E. G. Stokes to Secretary of Agriculture, 13 September 1920, General Correspondence of the Secretary of Agriculture, RG 16, NARA; E. G. Moss to J. H. Warren, 3 December 1920, Tobacco Growers' Cooperative Association Papers, SHC. The volume of tobacco marketed in Danville warehouses increased almost 84 percent from 1919 to 1920, while the average price per pound fell by more than half, from 55 cents to 26 cents. See Annual Market Statistics, President's Report, 1984, Reel 2, Records of the Danville Tobacco Association, Library of Virginia. For the post–World War I crisis in agriculture, see Tindall, *The Emergence of the New South, 1913–1945*, 111–42.

3. Tilley, *The Bright-Tobacco Industry*, 449–86; Woeste, *The Farmer's Benevolent Trust*, 196–202.

4. For farm women and the Tri-State, see Bennett, "'A Responsibility on Women That Cannot Be Delegated to Father, Husband, or Son,'" 67–96.

5. For Swanson's support, see Swanson to M. O. Wilson, 26 November 1921, Box 8, Papers of Claude A. Swanson, Albert and Shirley Small Special Collections Library, University of Virginia, Charlottesville.

6. Federal Writers' Project of North Carolina, "Gamblers All," 432, Charles Horace Hamilton Papers, SCRC.

7. Extension agent's report, 1922, Lunenburg County, Virginia, Extension Service Annual Narrative and Statistical Reports, RG 33.6, NARA. For a history of the Extension

Service and its connections to Progressive Era impulses to improve southern agriculture, see Grantham, *Southern Progressivism*, 333–42.

8. Editorial, *The Progressive Farmer*, 26 February 1921; "All the Big Men," *Tri-State Tobacco Grower*, June 1922; Bennett, "'A Responsibility on Women That Cannot Be Delegated to Father, Husband, or Son,'" 83–85.

9. Frissell, "Economic Co-Operation in Virginia," 435–36.

10. Negro Extension Service agent's report, 1922, Alamance County, North Carolina, Extension Service Annual Narrative and Statistical Reports, RG 33.6, NARA.

11. E.A. Jackson, letter to the editor, *Tri-State Tobacco Grower*, November 1924.

12. *The Progressive Farmer*, 29 January 1921; "A Million Have Gone," *Tri-State Tobacco Grower*, June 1922.

13. Mrs. Ed Carraway, letter to the editor, *Tri-State Tobacco Grower*, July 1922. In most instances references to women in the *Tri-State Tobacco Grower* use the title "Mrs." and do not include the woman's first name.

14. *Tri-State Tobacco Grower*, June 1924. For Mrs. Ferabee's reports, see *Tri-State Tobacco Grower*, March 1923 and July 1923.

15. "Program for T.G.C.A." submitted by Maude Barnard Browne, *Tri-State Tobacco Grower*, September 1924; Mrs. Mulchi, "Come to the Co-op Meeting," undated, Folder 67, Box 5, Tobacco Growers' Cooperative Association Papers, SHC.

16. *Tri-State Tobacco Grower*, August 1922; Lillie Smith, letter to the editor, *Tri-State Tobacco Grower*, August 1923.

17. Amy Harris to T. B. Young, *Tri-State Tobacco Grower*, September 1923; Mrs. W. E. Blankenship, letter to the editor, *Tri-State Tobacco Grower*, August 1925.

18. In 1925, the Danville Tobacco Association reported that the entire bright tobacco belt had produced 423,287,000 pounds of tobacco, of which an estimated 70,000,000 pounds had been delivered to the cooperative. See President's Report, 1925, Records of the Danville Tobacco Association, Library of Virginia.

19. Responses to Sydney Frissell surveys by James Fulton, 24 February 1928, and S. T. Morris, 1928, Tobacco Growers' Cooperative Association Papers, SHC. In 1928, Frissell mailed surveys to farmers who had been involved in the organization of the Tobacco Growers' Cooperative Association in the early 1920s in order to document the impact of the decline of the cooperative in 1925. "Narrative Report of the County Agent, 1929: Stokes County, North Carolina," Extension Service Annual Narrative and Statistical Reports, RG 33.6, NARA.

20. Response to Sydney Frissell survey by M. C. Johnson, Tobacco Growers' Cooperative Association Papers, SHC; "Narrative Report of the County Agent, 1927: Henry County Virginia," and "Narrative Report of the County Agent, 1935: Henry County, Virginia," Extension Service Annual Narrative and Statistical Reports, RG 33.6, NARA.

21. "Cooperation of All Is Basis of Tobacco Pool," *South Hill Enterprise*, 13 February 1930; "Will Not Pool This Year's Tobacco Crop," *South Hill Enterprise*, 2 April 1931; Badger, *Prosperity Road*, 29–31.

22. "Tobacco Sales Large, Much Leaf Type," *South Hill Enterprise*, 5 November 1931; "Call for Big Reduction in Tobacco Production," *South Hill Enterprise*, 12 November 1931; "Narrative Report of the County Agent, 1931: Stokes County, North Carolina," Extension Service Annual Narrative and Statistical Reports, RG 33.6, NARA. For background on these programs, see Badger, *Prosperity Road*, chapter 1.

23. For a detailed account of the design and implementation of the tobacco program, see Badger, *Prosperity Road*; and Pugh, "The Federal Tobacco Program: How It Works and Alternatives for Change," 13–29. Growers voted down controls on the 1939 crop because delays in the announcement of the 1938 quotas had created a great deal of confusion and frustration. The low prices that resulted from a large volume of tobacco in 1939 convinced growers to vote for the program in 1940, and they supported it in every subsequent referendum.

24. Badger, *Prosperity Road*, 45; J. S. Ray to Josiah W. Bailey, 9 February 1934, and M. O. Blount to Josiah W. Bailey, 10 February 1934, Josiah William Bailey Papers, David M. Rubenstein Rare Book and Manuscript Library, Duke University.

25. Tilley, *The Bright-Tobacco Industry*, 295–98; Woofter, *The Plight of Cigarette Tobacco*, 53; *South Hill Enterprise*, 10 October 1929.

26. "Report of the County Agent, 1929: Mecklenburg County, Virginia"; "Report of the County Agent, 1930 Vance County, North Carolina"; "Report of the County Agent, 1930: Orange County, North Carolina"; all in Extension Service Annual Narrative and Statistical Reports, RG 33.6, NARA.

27. *Danville Register* quoted in "Tobacco and the Politician," *South Hill Enterprise*, 10 November 1927.

28. Central Leaf Company to Josiah W. Bailey, 13 February 1935; C. W. Lea & Company to Josiah W. Bailey, 19 April 1934, Josiah William Bailey Papers, David M. Rubenstein Rare Book and Manuscript Library, Duke University; J. Con Lanier, "Why the Flanagan Compulsory Tobacco Grading Bill Should Not Be Enacted," undated published flyer (ca. 1935), Papers of Carter Glass, 1858–1946, Albert and Shirley Small Special Collections Library, University of Virginia, Charlottesville (hereafter Papers of Carter Glass).

29. A. E. Jackson to Josiah W. Bailey, 12 July 1935, and W. B. Jones to Josiah W. Bailey, 8 March 1935, Josiah William Bailey Papers, David M. Rubenstein Rare Book and Manuscript Library, Duke University; resolutions passed by officers of the Halifax County Farmers' Clubs and County and Community Tobacco Committees, 26 March 1935, Papers of Carter Glass; Mrs. Tom Merritt to Josiah W. Bailey, 23 February 1943, Josiah William Bailey Papers, David M. Rubenstein Rare Book and Manuscript Library, Duke University.

30. Badger, *Prosperity Road*, 179–80, 188–90; Pugh, "Landmarks in the Tobacco Program," 32.

31. "Narrative Report of the County Agent, 1936: Durham County, N.C.," Extension Service Annual Narrative and Statistical Reports, North Carolina, Reel 72, RG 33.6, NARA.

Chapter 5. Stabilization

1. Wrather, "Tobacco," 1, 4.

2. "A Burocrat's [sic] View of the Family Farm," *Chicago Tribune* 15 January 1963.

3. Flannagan quoted in Hardin, "The Tobacco Program: Exception or Portent?," 920.

4. "Narrative Report of the County Agent, 1935: Charlotte County, Virginia," Extension Service Annual Narrative and Statistical Reports, RG 33.6, NARA.

5. W. S. McKinney to Josiah Bailey, 18 May 1938; Myrtle S. Jones to Josiah Bailey, 29 November 1937; W. L. Spoon to Josiah Bailey, 11 December 1937, Josiah William Bailey Papers, David M. Rubenstein Rare Book and Manuscript Library, Duke University; C. M. Tyson to Harold Cooley, 14 November 1935, Harold Dunbar Cooley Papers, SHC.

6. Graham, *Improving Low Incomes on Tobacco Farms*, 54. From 1930 to 1940, the number of sharecroppers in the Old Bright Belt decreased from 40,189 to 33,863, a decline of 15.7 percent. Interestingly, the number of cash renters increased by over 24 percent during the same period. Some of these were sharecroppers who moved up the tenancy ladder, but most were likely landowners who simply rented additional land in order to get access to the allotment. Statistics compiled from 1930 and 1940 federal censuses, Historical Census Browser, University of Virginia, Geospatial and Statistical Data Center, http://mapserver.lib.virginia.edu. For sharecroppers' search for land, see, for example, Troy Britt to M. H. Jones, 25 November 1934, Harriet Smith to Eula Jones, 27 November 1934, and Troy Parrish to M. H. Jones, 10 December 1934, all in M. H. Jones Papers, SHC.

7. "Narrative Report of the County Agent, 1934: Stokes County, North Carolina," Extension Service Annual Narrative and Statistical Reports, RG 33.6, NARA; J. M. Judd to Josiah Bailey, 2 December 1937, Josiah William Bailey Papers, David M. Rubenstein Rare Book and Manuscript Library, Duke University; "Narrative Report of the County Agent, 1935: Pittsylvania County, Virginia," Extension Service Annual Narrative and Statistical Reports, RG 33.6, NARA; U.S. Department of Commerce, Bureau of the Census, *Census of Agriculture, 1935: Virginia*, Table 4; "Narrative Report of the County Agent, 1939: Forsyth County, North Carolina," Extension Service Annual Narrative and Statistical Reports, RG 33.6, NARA; Hagood, *Mothers of the South*, 82; Narrative Report of the County Agent (Negro), 1945: Durham County, North Carolina," Extension Service Annual Narrative and Statistical Reports, RG 33.6, NARA.

8. S. T. Dunn to Josiah Bailey, 2 January 1938, Josiah William Bailey Papers, David M. Rubenstein Rare Book and Manuscript Library, Duke University.

9. J. W. Powell to Josiah Bailey, 5 October 1942, Josiah William Bailey Papers, David M. Rubenstein Rare Book and Manuscript Library, Duke University.

10. "Narrative Report of the County Agent (Negro), 1943: Orange County, North Carolina," "Narrative Report of the County Agent, 1943: Durham County, North Carolina," Extension Service Annual Narrative and Statistical Reports, RG 33.6, NARA.

11. Quoted in "Narrative Report of the County Agent (Negro), 1944: Guilford

County, North Carolina," Extension Service Annual Narrative and Statistical Reports, North Carolina, RG 33.6, NARA.

12. J. L. Walker to Josiah Bailey, 4 January 1942, Josiah William Bailey Papers, David M. Rubenstein Rare Book and Manuscript Library, Duke University. "Narrative Report of the County Agent, 1942: Surry County, North Carolina," Extension Service Annual Narrative and Statistical Reports, RG 33.6, NARA; "Narrative Report of the County Agent, 1943: Davidson County, North Carolina," Extension Service Annual Narrative and Statistical Reports, RG 33.6, NARA.

13. "Narrative Report of the County Agent, 1943: Halifax County, Virginia," Extension Service Annual Narrative and Statistical Reports, RG 33.6, NARA.

14. For background on federal farm labor policy during the war, see Hahamovitch, *The Fruits of Their Labor*, chapter 7.

15. "Narrative Report of the County Agent, 1944: Caswell County, North Carolina," "Narrative Report of the County Agent, 1945: Caswell County, North Carolina," "Narrative Report of the County Agent, 1946: Caswell County, North Carolina," Extension Service Annual Narrative and Statistical Reports, RG 33.6, NARA.

16. "Narrative Report of the County Agent (Negro), 1942: Rockingham County, North Carolina," Extension Service Annual Narrative and Statistical Reports, RG 33.6, NARA. From 1933 to 1939, prices on the Danville market averaged just over 21 cents per pound; from 1940 to 1945, the average price was nearly 37 cents per pound, an increase of roughly 75 percent. By 1945, however, prices had increased to over 45 cents per pound, doubling some of the best years of the 1930s. Compiled from President's Report, 1984, Reel 2, Records of the Danville Tobacco Association, Library of Virginia.

17. "Report of the County Agent (Negro), 1946: Halifax County, Virginia," Extension Service Annual Narrative and Statistical Reports, RG 33.6, NARA. From 1940 to 1950, the number of owner-operated farms in Old Bright Belt counties in Virginia and North Carolina increased from 52,990 to 57,780 while the total number of farms decreased from 92,790 to 87,531. The decrease in the number tenant farms was more dramatic, over 23 percent, from 39,626 to 30,408. The steepest declines were in counties where the tenant population had either easy access to off-farm work or easy access to land or both. In Nottoway County, Virginia, for example, the decline in the number of tenant farms, which decreased by more than half during the decade (450 to 203), was largely due to people leaving for work on the nearby military installation or in Richmond and surrounding cities. Overall, the county lost 23 percent of its farms (1,595 to 1,226) and experienced a slight decrease in population (15,556 to 15,479). In Davidson County, the decline in tenancy was likely attributable to a combination of people taking public work and buying land. From 1940 to 1950, the number of tenant-operated farms decreased by nearly 60 percent (681 to 276) while the number of owner-operated farms increased by just over 19 percent (2,613 to 3,119). During the same period, the tenancy rate declined from 20.6 percent to 8.1 percent. Davidson County was a growing industrial center, and many landowners worked small tobacco crops on the side, successfully combining access to

off-farm work with access to land. All figures compiled from 1940 and 1950 censuses of population, Historical Census Browser, University of Virginia, Geospatial and Statistical Data Center, http://mapserver.lib.virginia.edu. For conditions in Davidson County, see "Report of the County Agent, 1958: Davidson County, North Carolina," Extension Service Annual Narrative and Statistical Reports, RG 33.6, NARA.

18. W. C. Gentry to Ezra Taft Benson, 11 August 1954, Tobacco Correspondence, Records of the Agricultural Stabilization and Conservation Agency, RG 145, NARA.

19. American Tobacco Company, "Chemicals Can Protect Flue-Cured Tobacco," in *Producing Finer Flue Cured Tobacco*, Box 2, Folder 23, John H. Hager Papers, VHS. This book includes a number of advertisements run by the American Tobacco Company from 1951–1956 designed to encourage tobacco farmers to adopt the latest agricultural technologies. "Deaths from DDT Successor Stir Concerns," *New York Times*, 21 August 1970; Daniel, *Toxic Drift*, 121–23.

20. For Farm Bureau support for the 1955 proposed cuts, see Carl T. Hicks to Carl Durham, 20 December 1955, Carl Thomas Durham Papers, SHC. Based on the recommendation of the Farm Bureau's Flue-Cured Tobacco Advisory Committee, Hicks, the chair of the North Carolina bureau, pressed Representative Durham to support the cuts, arguing that "tobacco growers who want to keep our tobacco program sound" would support the cuts.

21. Aubrey W. Henry to Ezra Taft Benson, 8 January 1959; Clyde Tate to Ezra Taft Benson, 18 February 1959, Tobacco Correspondence, Records of the Agricultural Stabilization and Conservation Agency, RG 145, NARA.

22. Bishop, Henry, and Finkner, *Underplanting Tobacco Allotments*, 2. In North Carolina's northern Piedmont counties, 7.3 percent of farms with allotments planted no tobacco in 1953. The counties with above-average percentages of farms with unplanted allotments (Forsyth, 21.8; Yadkin, 12.4; Guilford, 11.4; Durham, 11.2) were the most urbanized, while those with the lowest percentages of farms with unplanted allotments (Person, 0.8; Caswell, 1.5; Granville, 1.6; Vance, 1.6) were among the most rural and remote. Not all growers in these rural counties were growing on their own allotments, but many found more opportunity to rent their land to other growers who wanted to expand their acreages. In some of the more urbanized counties, much of the land was sold for development, so while the allotment remained attached to the land until it was absorbed by the Agricultural Stabilization and Conservation Agency for redistribution, there was little chance it would be used. The Old Belt had much higher percentages of unplanted allotments than other regions. The same study found that in North Carolina counties outside the northern Piedmont, only 4.3 percent of farms with allotments had no tobacco planted. H. A. Bennett to Carl Durham, 30 January 1950, Carl Thomas Durham Papers, SHC; Pasour, McPherson, and Toussaint, *Economic Opportunities for Adjustments on Tobacco Farms in the Northern Piedmont, North Carolina*, 5, 14, 17; "Report of the County Agent, 1957: Lunenburg County, Virginia," Extension Service Annual Narrative and Statistical Reports, RG 33.6, NARA. The number of Old Bright Belt farm operators decreased from 89,283 in 1945 to 51,773 in 1964. Compiled from U.S. Department of Commerce, Bureau of

the Census, *Census of Agriculture: 1945*, Volume 1, Parts 15 and 16; and U.S. Department of Commerce, Bureau of the Census, *1964 Census of Agriculture*, Parts 24 and 26.

23. Wadley and Lee, "The Disappearance of the Black Farmer," 280–81; Schulman and Newman, "The Survival of the Black Tobacco Farmer," 46–52; VISTA Report from Halifax County, Virginia, 5 August 1968, Folder 42, Box 63, National Sharecroppers Fund Records, Walter P. Reuther Library, Wayne State University; Bryant Miller to Secretary of Agriculture, 16 September 1959, Tobacco Correspondence, Records of the Agricultural Stabilization and Conservation Agency, RG 145, NARA, italics in original; Daniel, *Dispossession*.

24. Pasour, McPherson, and Toussaint, *Economic Opportunities for Adjustments on Tobacco Farms in the Northern Piedmont, North Carolina*, 10; "Report of the County Agent, 1958: Davidson County, North Carolina," Extension Service Annual Narrative and Statistical Reports, RG 33.6, NARA. Figures on household income contributions from U.S. Department of Commerce, Bureau of the Census, *1964 Census of Agriculture*, Parts 24 (Virginia) and 26 (North Carolina), Tables 4 and 7. Of the 51,773 Old Bright Belt farm operators, 20,306 reported working of the farm themselves while 22,482 reported that other members of the household contributed to the family finances. Sutherland, *The Effects of Tobacco Prices and Allotment Variations on Farm Organizations and Incomes, Northern Piedmont Area, North Carolina*, 12. Sutherland's claim was based on 1964 data that showed that 81 percent of the region's farms had less than $10,000 in farm sales and over half had less than $5,000; U.S. Department of Commerce, Bureau of the Census, *1964 Census of Agriculture*, Parts 24 (Virginia) and 26 (North Carolina), Tables 4 and 7 . Of the region's 51,773 operators, 42,788 reported that either they or a family member worked off the farm.

25. Schapsmeier and Schapsmeier, "Farm Policy from FDR to Eisenhower," 355; political advertisement, *Spring Hope Enterprise*, 29 October 1964.

26. Schapsmeier and Schapsmeier, "Farm Policy from FDR to Eisenhower," 355. "Burley Acreage Face Cut of 15%" and "Other Quotas Reduced" *New York Times*, 1 December 1955; "Benson Hails End of Corn Controls," *New York Times*, 27 November 1958; "Nixon and Benson Get Wire Crossed," *New York Times*, 9 September 1960.

27. "Growers Vote to Keep Strict Marketing Quotas," *New York Times*, 17 December 1958; "Truman Campaigns through Carolina," *New York Times*, 15 October 1960.

28. "Annual Report—13th Stockholders Meeting, Flue-Cured Tobacco Cooperative Stabilization Corporation, June 26, 1959," Tobacco Correspondence, Records of the Agricultural Stabilization and Conservation Agency, RG 145, NARA.

29. Ibid.

30. Ibid.

31. Agricultural Stabilization and Conservation Service, *Identification of Certain Flue-Cured Tobacco Varieties under the Price Support Program*, 3–5.

32. U.S. Environmental Protection Agency, *Maleic Hydrazide*. For the health risks related to MH-30, see Daniel, *Toxic Drift*, 124; "Governor's Proposal Favored," *Greensboro Daily News*, 27 November 1962; "U.S. Tobacco Program, Once Praised as Model, Runs into Troubles," *Wall Street Journal*, 14 February 1963.

33. "Report of the County Agent, 1954: Guilford County, North Carolina," Extension Service Annual Narrative and Statistical Reports, RG 33.6, NARA; "Troubles Beset Tobacco Areas," *New York Times*, 4 October 1964; "Annual Report—13th Stockholders Meeting, Flue-Cured Tobacco Cooperative Stabilization Corporation, June 26, 1959"; "U.S. Tobacco Program, Once Praised as Model, Runs into Troubles."

34. "Annual Report—13th Stockholders Meeting, Flue-Cured Tobacco Cooperative Stabilization Corporation, June 26, 1959."

35. E. Y. Floyd to Joe R. Williams, 16 October 1959, Tobacco Correspondence, Records of the Agricultural Stabilization and Conservation Agency, RG 145, NARA.

36. U.S. Department of Agriculture, Agricultural Research Service, "The Effects of Maleic Hydrazide on the Suitability of Tobacco for Cigarette Manufacture," April 1961, Legacy Tobacco Documents Library, http://legacy.library.ucsf.edu/tid/luj13c00/pdf.

37. John H. Brown to Horace Kornegay, 27 November 1962, Horace Kornegay Papers, SHC; "Governor's Proposal Favored," *Greensboro Daily News*, 27 November 1962.

38. "Memorandum of Use of MH-30 on Tobacco," Horace Kornegay Papers, n.d.; John C. Williamson to Horace Kornegay, 8 March 1963, Horace Kornegay Papers.

39. John C. Williamson to Horace Kornegay, 8 March 1963; "Memorandum of Use of MH-30 on Tobacco"; Lawrence Wells to L. Y. Ballentine, 22 January 1963, General Correspondence, L. Y. Ballentine Papers, State Archives of North Carolina, Raleigh.

40. "Report of the County Agent, 1958: Guilford County, North Carolina," Extension Service Annual Narrative and Statistical Reports, RG 33.6, NARA.

41. Minutes of Sucker Control Advisory Committee Meeting, 24 March 1964, Raleigh, North Carolina, Legacy Tobacco Documents Library, http://legacy.library.ucsf.edu/tid/eza43d00/pdf.

42. "Sucker Control Committee Discussion of Epstein Work," Brown & Williamson Internal Memo, April 1967, Legacy Tobacco Documents Library, http://legacy.library.ucsf.edu/tid/fcy40f00/pdf; "Maleic Hydrazide: Mammalian Toxicity and Suggested Carcinogenicity," American Tobacco Company Internal Memo, n.d., Legacy Tobacco Documents Library, http://legacy.library.ucsf.edu/tid/jht54f00/pdf.

43. Hill and Knowlton Informational Memo, 29 September 1967, Legacy Tobacco Documents Library, http://legacy.library.ucsf.edu/tid/dsc34f00/pdf.

Chapter 6. Untied

1. "Short-Lived Impact Is Predicted Here," *Winston-Salem Journal*, 12 January 1964; "Report on Smoking Disturbs but Does Not Panic Tobaccoland," *Danville Register*, 12 January 1964; Brandt, *The Cigarette Century*, 237.

2. "Meeting with Old Bright Belt Growers, South Hill, Virginia, April 2, 1968," American Tobacco Company Meeting Minutes, Legacy Tobacco Documents Library, http://legacy.library.ucsf.edu/tid/bqq80a00/pdf.

3. Mann, *Tobacco*, 61–62.

4. In 1969, estimates from North Carolina indicated that mechanical harvesters cost between $3,500 and $4,500, a tobacco-stringing machine known as a looper cost between $1,400 and $2,000, and bulk curing barns cost roughly $3,000 each. During this time, tobacco brought in an average of $72.79 per hundred pounds. See "Tobacco Farming: A Harvest of Woe," *New York Times*, 6 October 1969.

5. Mann, "The Tobacco Franchise for Whom?," 40; Mann, *Tobacco*, 1; Siceloff, "Tobacco in Transition," 47; U.S. Department of Agriculture Economic Research Service, *Direct and Contract Hiring of Seasonal Farm Labor*, 4–5. Using 1966 statistics, the Economic Research Service report found that nearly 90 percent of those hiring farm labor directly hired the workers, indicating that many seasonal workers were hired individually or as families. Tellingly, nearly half also went through labor contractors, likely indicating an increased reliance on migrant workers brought in by labor bosses.

6. Virginia Employment Commission, *Virginia Annual Farm Labor Report: 1964*, 8. In this case, the Virginia Employment Commission and the local Sertoma Club had sponsored the job fair that signed up the teenagers; Virginia Employment Commission, *Virginia Annual Farm Labor Report, 1970*, 13. In some ways, this program was very much like other migrant labor programs overseen by the state. Growers had to build state-approved dormitories for the teenagers and agree to pay them a certain wage. However, they also had to supervise the workers outside work. The program continued for at least three seasons. "Leaf Work Beats Homework," *News & Observer* (Raleigh, N.C.), 22 August 1974; Virginia Employment Commission, *Virginia Annual Rural Manpower Report, 1973*, 8; Mann, *Tobacco*, 11.

7. L. Cyrus Snipes to Ike Andrews, 28 August 1973, Ike Franklin Andrews Papers, SHC; "Farmers Count More on Migrant Laborers," *Durham Morning Herald*, 11 August 1976. According to the *Herald* article, almost 75 percent of the migrant workers were Spanish speakers, mostly of Mexican descent.

8. "Farmers Learn New Language," *Winston-Salem Journal and Sentinel*, 4 May 1975. In this instance, most of the growers attending the class wanted to learn common phrases needed for tobacco work (e.g. "Do you know how to sucker tobacco?"), but this desire to overcome the language barrier, even at the smallest level, indicated that some growers were not yet ready to cede control over the labor in their fields.

9. In 1983, North Carolina officials estimated that only 25 percent of migrant workers had been placed by the state employment board while about 60 percent worked for freewheeling crews; Legislative Research Commission, *Migrant Workers: Report to the 1983 General Assembly of North Carolina*, 14, 29; "Itinerant Workers Held Against Their Will?," *Greensboro Daily News*, 20 August 1981. For background on the conditions of migrant farm labor in North Carolina, see U.S. Commission on Civil Rights, *Where Mules Outrate Men*.

10. "Mexican Laborers in Virginia Reap a Whirlwind," *Washington Post*, 23 May 1983. This report indicated that from 1980 to 1982, Virginia growers had imported between 1,200 and 1,500 workers and that another 863 were expected during the 1983 season. These

workers, the report claimed, filled about one-fourth of the available tobacco jobs. Wasem and Colliver, *Immigration of Agricultural Guest Workers.*

11. "Mexican Laborers in Virginia Reap a Whirlwind"; "Golden Leaf Brings Many to Southside," *Richmond Times Dispatch,* 10 November 1996.

12. Yeoman, "Silence in the Fields," 43

13. Ibid., 83; "N.C. Farmworkers Sue Growers Association, Charge Blacklisting," Associated Press Wire Report, 20 April 2004.

14. "N.C. Farmworkers Sue Growers Association, Charge Blacklisting."

15. Bacon, "Be Our Guests."

16. Oxfam America, *A State of Fear.*

Chapter 7. Buyout

1. I attended the St. Paul's meeting on 8 April 2005. See also "Farmers Seek Buyout Answers," *Richmond Times-Dispatch,* 10 April 2005. For the stipulations of the buyout, see American Jobs Creation Act of 2004, Title VI, http://www.gpo.gov/fdsys/pkg/PLAW-108publ357/pdf/PLAW-108publ357.pdf; and "Growers 'Look Beyond' Tobacco Crop," *Southeast Farm Press,* 20 April 2005.

2. "Congress Readying Tobacco Buyout," *The Washington Times,* 2 April 2004.

3. Johnny D. Braden, "Economic Analysis of Tobacco Quota Transfers," paper delivered at the National Tobacco Advisory Committee Meeting, 15 November 1972, Harry Flood Byrd, Jr. Papers, Albert and Shirley Small Special Collections Library, University of Virginia, Charlottesville (hereafter Harry Flood Byrd, Jr. Papers); Mann, *Tobacco,* 32–35.

4. Mann, *Tobacco,* 32–35.

5. Jesse R. Edmonds to Ike Andrews, 23 January 1973, and Ike Andrews to Jesse Edmonds, 12 February 1973, both in Ike Franklin Andrews Papers, SHC; Mann, *Tobacco,* 12.

6. Ike Andrews to Earl Butz, 4 August 1975, Ike Franklin Andrews Papers, SHC; Logan Finch to Harry Flood Byrd, Jr., 19 August 1975, Harry Flood Byrd, Jr., Papers.

7. "Farmers Claim Industry Pressured Increases in Flue Quotas," *Tobacco Reporter,* February 1974, 14.

8. J. R. Yates to Harry F. Byrd, Jr., 1 January 1974; Jerry L. Martin to Harry F. Byrd, Jr., 28 December 1973; and Regina M. Crawley to William L. Lanier, 2 January 1974, all in Harry Flood Byrd, Jr., Papers.

9. Mann, *Tobacco,* 21, 46–47; "Tobacco Growers Fear for Future amid Drive to End Price Supports," *New York Times,* 20 July 1977.

10. Resolution of the City Council, South Boston, Va., 6 February 1978, Harry Flood Byrd, Jr., Papers; "Carter Vows to Help Tobacco Farmers," *Los Angeles Times,* 6 August 1978.

11. President's Report, 1979, 3–4, Records of the Danville Tobacco Association, Library of Virginia.

12. Parker-Pope, *Cigarettes,* 109–24.

13. Ibid., 113–24.

14. Ibid. For the breakup of the Tobacco Institute, see "Multistate Settlement with the Tobacco Industry," Legacy Tobacco Documents Library, http://legacy.library.ucsf.edu /tid/jwo08c00/pdf.

15. Certificate of Incorporation, Tobacco Growers' Information Committee, November 1958, Raleigh, North Carolina, Legacy Tobacco Documents Library, http://legacy .library.ucsf.edu/tid/lmw5aa00/pdf.

16. Tobacco Institute press release, 20 December 1958, Legacy Tobacco Documents Library, http://legacy.library.ucsf.edu/tid/pjf91f00.pdf. A financial statement from FY 1967 showed that the matching $25,000 donations the Tobacco Institute and Tobacco Associates, Inc., gave to the TGIC provided about 95 percent of its total revenues. See Quarterly Statement, October 31, 1966–January 31, 1967, Tobacco Growers' Information Committee, Inc., Legacy Tobacco Documents Library, http://legacy.library.ucsf.edu /tid/ccj04f00/pdf.

17. Tobacco Institute Advertisements, 1978, Legacy Tobacco Documents Library, http://legacy.library.ucsf.edu/tid/nuu92f00/pdf; Benson, *Tobacco Capitalism,* 108–12.

18. William Curtis Randolph to Harry F. Byrd, 20 August 1975, Harry F. Byrd, Jr., Papers; Henry Ferrell, "Ode to a Tobacco Farmer," 1975, Box 3, Folder 72, Ike Franklin Andrews Papers, SHC.

19. Daniel, *Breaking the Land,* 267, 269–70; "Senate Defeats Move to End Sugar Subsidies," *New York Times,* 18 September 1981; Womach, "Tobacco Price Support: An Overview of the Program," 4. Peter Benson offers one of the best overviews of the politics of the tobacco program in the years after 1980; Benson, *Tobacco Capitalism,* 97–131.

20. Benson, *Tobacco Capitalism,* 99–101.

21. Ibid., 104–6.

22. "Rebuffs Rep. Rose: Grange Rejects Tobacco Buyout," *Star-News* (Wilmington, N.C.), 26 October 1994.

23. "As Tobacco Slumps, Warehouses Close," *News & Observer* (Raleigh, N.C.), 3 August 2000; "Opening Up the Bids," *Winston-Salem Journal,* 7 August 2002; "Tobacco Auction Warehouses: Going, Going . . . ," *Richmond Times-Dispatch,* 6 November 2001; "R. J. Reynolds Settles Lawsuit," *Richmond Times-Dispatch,* 23 April 2004.

Conclusion

1. 2007 Census of Agriculture, Volume 1, Chapter 2, Table 2, http://www.agcensus .usda.gov/Publications/2007/Full_Report/Volume_1,_Chapter_2_County_Level/.

2. Benson, *Tobacco Capitalism,* 135–65.

3. Bennett, "Manning the Fields," 736–37; Benson, *Tobacco Capitalism,* 166–210.

Bibliography

Primary Sources

Archival Collections

Albert and Shirley Small Special Collections Library, University of Virginia, Charlottesville

Papers of Harry Flood Byrd, Jr.
Papers of Carter Glass, 1845–1946
Claude A. Swanson Papers

David M. Rubenstein Rare Book and Manuscript Library, Duke University, Durham, North Carolina

Josiah William Bailey Papers, 1833–1967
Thomas Carroll Papers, 1844–1914
Samuel C. Hubbard Papers

Library of Virginia, Richmond

Records of the Danville Tobacco Association
Leftwich-Shepherd Bowles Family Papers

National Archives and Records Administration (NARA), Washington, D.C.

Records of the Bureau of Refugees, Freedmen, and Abandoned Lands, Record Group 105

National Archives and Records Administration (NARA), College Park, Maryland

Records of the Extension Service, Annual Narrative and Statistical Reports, Record Group 33.6
Records of the Agricultural Stabilization and Conservation Agency, Record Group 145
Records of the Office of the Secretary of Agriculture, General Correspondence, Record Group 16

North Carolina Collection, University of North Carolina Chapel Hill Libraries

Clipping File through 1975
Johnson, Elmer D. "Life on a Tobacco Farm in the 1920's." Unpublished manuscript.

Southern Historical Collection (SHC), University of North Carolina, Chapel Hill

Ike Franklin Andrews Papers
Harold Dunbar Cooley Papers
Carl Thomas Durham Papers
Federal Writers' Project Papers
M. H. Jones Papers
Horace Kornegay Papers
L. L. Polk Papers
Southern Oral History Program Collection
Stockard, Sallie Walker. "Daughter of the Piedmont." Manuscript.
Tobacco Growers' Cooperative Association Papers
Zebulon Baird Vance Papers
William Wallace White Diaries

Special Collections Research Center (SCRC), North Carolina State University, Raleigh

Charles Horace Hamilton Papers

State Archives of North Carolina, Raleigh

L. Y. Ballentine Papers

Virginia Historical Society (VHS), Richmond

Burwell Family Papers
John H. Hager Papers
Hannah Family Papers
Miller Family Papers

Walter P. Reuther Library, Wayne State University, Detroit, Michigan

National Sharecroppers Fund Records

Interviews with the Author

William Hawthorne, May 2, 2003, Williamsburg, Virginia
H. G. Jones, May 14, 2003, Chapel Hill, North Carolina

Secondary Sources

Agricultural Stabilization and Conservation Service. *Identification of Certain Flue-Cured Tobacco Varieties under the Price Support Program*. Washington D.C.: U.S. Department of Agriculture, 1964.

Ali, Omar H. *In the Lion's Mouth: Black Populism in the New South, 1886–1900*. Jackson: University Press of Mississippi, 2010.

Andrews, Jesse. *Thirteen Month Crop: One Year in the Life of a Piedmont Virginia Tobacco Farm*. Durham: Center for Documentary Studies, 2003.

Ayers, Edward L. *The Promise of the New South: Life after Reconstruction*. New York: Oxford University Press, 1992.

Bacon, David. "Be Our Guests." *The Nation* 279 (27 September 2004): 22–28

Badger, Anthony J. *Prosperity Road: The New Deal, Tobacco, and North Carolina*. Chapel Hill: University of North Carolina Press, 1980.

Banks, Ann. "Tobacco Talk." *Southern Exposure* 8 (Winter 1980): 40–41.

Barefoot, Pamela, and Burt Kornegay. *Mules and Memories: A Photo Documentary of the Tobacco Farmer*. Winston-Salem, N.C.: John F. Blair, 1978.

Barrett, Charles Simon. *The Mission, History and Times of the Farmers' Union: A History of the Greatest Industrial-Agricultural Organization in History and Its Makers*. Nashville: Marshall & Bruce, 1909.

Beeby, James M. *Revolt of the Tar Heels: The North Carolina Populist Movement, 1890–1901*. Jackson: University Press of Mississippi, 2008.

Bennett, Evan P. "'A Responsibility on Women That Cannot Be Delegated to Father, Husband, or Son': Farm Women and Cooperation in the Tobacco South." In *Work, Family, and Faith: Rural Southern Women in the Twentieth Century*, edited by Melissa Walker and Rebecca Sharpless. Columbia: University of Missouri Press, 2006.

———. "Dubious Heritage: Tobacco, History, and the Perils of Remembering the Rural Past." *Agricultural History* 86 (Spring 2012): 23–40.

———. "Manning the Fields: Remaking Women's Work in the Tobacco South in the Twentieth Century." *Journal of Peasant Studies* 35 (October 2008): 720–41.

———. "Of the Quest of the Golden Leaf: Black Farmers and Bright Tobacco in the Piedmont South." In *Beyond Forty Acres and a Mule: African American Landowning Families since Reconstruction*, edited by Debra A Reid and Evan P. Bennett. Gainesville: University Press of Florida, 2012.

Benson, Peter. *Tobacco Capitalism: Growers, Migrant Workers, and the Changing Face of a Global Industry*. Princeton, N.J.: Princeton University Press, 2012.

Berry, Wendell. "Our Tobacco Problem." *The Progressive* 56 (May 1992): 17–19.

Birdsall, Stephen S. "Tobacco Farmers and Landscape Change in North Carolina's Old Belt Region." *Southeastern Geographer* 41 (May 2001): 65–73.

Bishop, C. E., W. R. Henry, and A. L. Finkner. *Underplanting Tobacco Allotments: Factors Affecting Tobacco Planting Decisions in Forsyth County and the Northern Piedmont*. Agricultural Economics Information Series 42. Raleigh: North Carolina State College, 1955.

Bolton, Charles C. *Poor Whites of the Antebellum South: Tenants and Laborers in Central North Carolina and Northeast Mississippi.* Durham, N.C.: Duke University Press, 1994.

Bradsher, A. B. "Tobacco Culture and Manufacture in North Carolina, part 1." *The Trinity Archive* 18 (April 1905): 379–88.

———. "Tobacco Culture and Manufacture in North Carolina, part 2." *The Trinity Archive* 18 (May 1905): 290–301.

Brandt, Allen. *The Cigarette Century: The Rise, Fall, and Deadly Persistence of the Product That Defined America.* New York: Basic Books, 2009.

Breen, T. H. *Tobacco Culture: The Mentality of the Great Tidewater Planters on the Eve of Revolution.* Princeton, N.J.: Princeton University Press, 1985.

Brooks, Jerome E. *Green Leaf and Gold: Tobacco in North Carolina.* Raleigh: North Carolina Department of Archives and History, 1962.

Browder, Nathaniel C. *The Tri-State Tobacco Growers Association, 1922–1925: The Co-Op That Failed.* 1940; repr., Raleigh: N. C. Browder, 1983.

Bruce, Philip A. *The Plantation Negro as a Freeman: Observations on His Character, Condition, and Prospects in Virginia.* New York: G. P. Putnam's Sons, 1889.

Buck, Solon J. *The Granger Movement: A Study of Agricultural Organization and Its Political, Economic, and Social Manifestations, 1870–1880.* 1913; repr., Lincoln: University of Nebraska Press, 1963.

Cameron, J. D. *A Sketch of the Tobacco Interests in North Carolina.* Oxford, N.C.: W. A. Davis, 1881.

Campbell, Tracy. *The Politics of Despair: Power & Resistance in the Tobacco Wars.* Lexington: University Press of Kentucky, 1993.

Censer, Jane Turner. *The Reconstruction of White Southern Womanhood, 1865–1895.* Baton Rouge: Louisiana State University Press, 2003.

Childress, Linda Hamlett. *A Tobacco Farmer's Daughter.* N.p.: 1stBooks, 2002.

Cohen, William. *At Freedom's Edge: Black Mobility and the Southern White Quest for Racial Control, 1861–1915.* Baton Rouge: Louisiana State University Press, 1991.

Creech, Joe. *Righteous Indignation: Religion & the Populist Revolution.* Urbana: University of Illinois Press, 2006.

Dailey, Jane. *Before Jim Crow: The Politics of Race in Postemancipation Virginia.* Chapel Hill: University of North Carolina Press, 2000.

Daniel, Pete. *Breaking the Land: The Transformation of Cotton, Tobacco, and Rice Cultures since 1880.* Urbana: University of Illinois Press, 1985.

———. *Dispossession: Discrimination against African American Farmers in the Age of Civil Rights.* Chapel Hill: University of North Carolina Press, 2013.

———. *Toxic Drift: Pesticides and Health in the Post–World War II South.* Baton Rouge: Louisiana State University Press, 2005.

Edwards, Laura F. *Gendered Strife and Confusion: The Political Culture of Reconstruction.* Urbana: University of Illinois Press, 1997.

Erickson, Franklin C. "The Tobacco Belt of North Carolina." *Economic Geography* 21 (January 1945): 58–61.

Fite, Gilbert. *Cotton Fields No More: Southern Agriculture, 1865–1980*. Lexington: University Press of Kentucky, 1984.

Fitzpatrick, Robert J. "Language of the Tobacco Market." *American Speech* 15 (April 1940): 132–35.

Flannagan, Roy C. "Virginia Tobacco." Richmond: Virginia State Chamber of Commerce. Reprint from *The Richmond News Leader*, n.d.

Foner, Philip S., and Ronald L. Lewis, eds. *The Black Worker: A Documentary History from Colonial Times to the Present*. Volume 3: *The Black Worker during the Era of the Knights of Labor*. Philadelphia: Temple University Press, 1978.

Frissell, Sydney D. "Economic Co-Operation in Virginia." *Southern Workman* 50 (October 1921): 435–36.

Garlock, Jonathan, comp. *Guide to the Local Assemblies of the Knights of Labor*. Westport, Conn.: Greenwood Press, 1982.

Garner, Bob. *North Carolina Barbecue: Flavored by Time*. Winston-Salem, N.C.: John F. Blair, 1996.

Graham, Robert E. *Improving Low Incomes on Tobacco Farms: Caswell County, North Carolina*. Washington, D.C.: U.S. Department of Agriculture, 1941.

Grantham, Dewey W. *Southern Progressivism: The Reconciliation of Progress and Tradition*. Knoxville: University of Tennessee Press, 1983.

Hagood, Margaret Jarman. *Mothers of the South: Portraiture of the White Tenant Farm Women*. Chapel Hill: University of North Carolina Press, 1939.

Hahamovitch, Cindy. *The Fruits of Their Labor: Atlantic Coast Farmworkers and the Making of Migrant Poverty, 1870–1945*. Chapel Hill: University of North Carolina Press, 1997.

———. *No Man's Land: Jamaican Guestworkers in America and the Global History of Deportable Labor*. Princeton, N.J.: Princeton University Press, 2011.

Hahn, Barbara. *Making Tobacco Bright: Creating an American Commodity, 1617–1937*. Baltimore, Md.: Johns Hopkins University Press, 2011.

———. "Into the Belly of the Beast: The 2002 North Carolina Flue-Cured Tobacco Tour." *Southern Cultures* 9 (Fall 2003): 25–50.

Hahn, Steven, Steven F. Miller, Susan E. O'Donovan, John Rodrigue, and Leslie S. Rowland, eds. *Freedom: A Documentary History of Emancipation, 1861–1867*. Series 3, Volume 1, *Land and Labor, 1865*. Chapel Hill: University of North Carolina Press, 2008.

Hall, Jacquelyn Dowd. *Like a Family: The Making of a Southern Cotton Mill World*. Chapel Hill: University of North Carolina Press, 1987.

Hardin, Charles M. "The Tobacco Program: Exception or Portent?" *Journal of Farm Economics* 28 (November 1946): 920–37.

Harris, Abram D. *The Negro as Capitalist: A Study of Banking and Business among American Negroes*. Philadelphia: American Academy of Political and Social Science, 1936.

Hart, John Fraser, and Ennis L. Chestang. "Turmoil in Tobaccoland." *The Geographical Review* 86 (October 1996): 550–72.

Hart, John Fraser, and Eugene Cotton Mather. "The Character of Tobacco Barns and Their Role in the Tobacco Economy of the United States." *Annals of the Association of American Geographers* 51 (September 1961): 274–93.

Hollander, Gail M. *Raising Cane in the 'Glades: The Global Sugar Trade and the Transformation of Florida.* Chicago: University of Chicago Press, 2008.

Holt, Sharon Ann. *Making Freedom Pay: North Carolina Freedpeople Working for Themselves, 1865–1900.* Athens: University of Georgia Press, 2000.

Hunter, J. B. *Useful Information Concerning Yellow Tobacco, and Other Crops, as Told by Forty of the Most Successful Farmers of Granville County, North Carolina.* Oxford, N.C.: W. A. Davis, 1880.

Janiewski, Dolores. *Sisterhood Denied: Race, Gender, and Class in a New South Community.* Philadelphia: Temple University Press, 1985.

Jones, A. O. "Bank Loans in North Carolina in 1915." In *The University of North Carolina Record* 149. Raleigh: Edwards & Broughton, 1917.

Kerr-Ritchie, Jeffrey R. *Freedpeople in the Tobacco South: Virginia, 1860–1900.* Chapel Hill: University of North Carolina Press, 1999.

Killebrew, J. B. *Report on the Culture and Curing of Tobacco in the United States.* Washington, D.C.: Government Printing Office, 1884.

Killebrew, J. B., and Herbert Myrick. *Tobacco Leaf: Its Culture and Cure, Marketing and Manufacture.* New York: Orange Judd, 1916.

Kirby, Jack Temple. *Rural Worlds Lost: The American South, 1920–1960.* Baton Rouge: Louisiana State University Press, 1987.

Knapp, John L. *Tobacco in Virginia.* Charlottesville: Weldon Cooper Center for Public Service, 1995.

Kulikoff, Allan. *Tobacco and Slaves: The Development of Southern Cultures in the Chesapeake, 1680–1800.* Chapel Hill: University of North Carolina Press, 1986.

Landon, Charles E. "The Tobacco Growing Industry in North Carolina," *Economic Geography* 10, no. 3 (July 1934): 239–53.

Langhorne, Orra. *Southern Sketches from Virginia, 1881–1901.* Edited by Charles E. Wynes. Charlottesville: University Press of Virginia, 1964.

Lasley, Robert T., and Sallie Holt, eds. *A Prayer for the Baby Goat and Other Alamance County Tales: A Treasury of 20th Century Memories.* Hickory, N.C.: Hometown Memories, 2001.

Legislative Research Commission (North Carolina). *Migrant Workers: Report of the 1983 General Assembly of North Carolina.* Raleigh, N.C.: Legislative Research Commission, 1983.

Leighton, Clare. *Southern Harvest.* New York: Macmillan, 1942).

Let's Talk Tobacco. Durham, N.C.: Center for Documentary Studies, 1998.

Loomis, Charles P. "The Rise and Decline of the North Carolina Farmers' Union." *North Carolina Historical Review* 7 (July 1930): 305–25.

Mann, Charles Kellogg. "The Tobacco Franchise for Whom?" In *The Tobacco Industry in Transition: Policies for the 1980s*, edited by William Finger. Lexington, Mass.: Lexington Books, 1981.

———. *Tobacco: The Ants and the Elephants.* Salt Lake City: Olympus, 1975.

Marshall, Suzanne. *Violence in the Black Patch of Kentucky and Tennessee.* Columbia: University of Missouri Press, 1994.

Marti, Donald B. *Women of the Grange: Mutuality and Sisterhood in Rural America, 1866–1920.* New York: Greenwood Press, 1991.

McMath, Robert C., Jr. *Populist Vanguard: A History of the Southern Farmers' Alliance.* Chapel Hill: University of North Carolina Press, 1975.

Morgan, Lynda J. *Emancipation in Virginia's Tobacco Belt, 1850–1870.* Athens: University of Georgia Press, 1992.

Munroe, Kirk. "Danville, Virginia." *Harper's Weekly* 31 (29 January 1887): 75.

National Farmers' Union. *Constitution and By-Laws of the Farmers Educational and Co-Operative Union of America, Virginia Division, Adopted December 6, 1917.* Bedford, Va.: Bedford Imprint, 1917.

National Grange. *Manual of the Subordinate Granges of the Patrons of Husbandry.* 9th ed. Philadelphia: George S. Ferguson Co., 1908.

Newby, I. A. *Plain Folk in the New South: Social Change and Cultural Persistence, 1880–1915.* Baton Rouge: Louisiana State University Press, 1989.

North Carolina. Department of Labor and Printing. *Thirtieth Annual Report of the Department of Labor and Printing of the State of State of North Carolina.* Raleigh, N.C.: Edwards and Broughton, 1916.

Orrell, Angela M. *From the Seed to the Hand: A Photographic Documentary of People of Tobacco.* Richmond: Virginia Museum of Fine Arts, 2005.

Ownby, Ted. *Subduing Satan: Religion, Recreation, & Manhood in the Rural South, 1865–1920.* Chapel Hill: University of North Carolina Press, 1990.

Oxfam America. *A State of Fear: Human Rights Abuses in North Carolina's Tobacco Industry.* Boston: Oxfam America, 2011. http://www.oxfamamerica.org/static/media/files/a-state-of-fear.pdf.

Parker-Pope, Tara. *Cigarettes: Anatomy of an Industry from Seed to Smoke.* New York: The New Press, 2001.

Pasour, E. C., W. W. McPherson, and W. Toussaint. *Economic Opportunities for Adjustments on Tobacco Farms in the Northern Piedmont, North Carolina.* Agricultural Economics Information Series 70. Raleigh: North Carolina State College, 1959.

Pasour, E. C., W. D. Toussaint, and G. S. Tolley. *North Carolina Piedmont and Coastal Plain Tobacco Farms: Their Changing Characteristics, 1955–1958.* Agricultural Economics Information Series 71. Raleigh: North Carolina State College, 1959.

Perman, Michael. *The Road to Redemption: Southern Politics, 1869–1879*. Chapel Hill: University of North Carolina Press, 1985.

Phillips, Anne Radford. "Farm Women of Stokes County, North Carolina, and the Production of Flue-Cured Tobacco, 1925–1955." PhD diss., University of Maryland, College Park, 1990.

Postel, Charles. *The Populist Vision*. Oxford: Oxford University Press, 2007.

Prince, Eldred E., and Robert R. Simpson. *Long Green: The Rise and Fall of Tobacco in South Carolina*. Athens: University of Georgia Press, 2000.

Ragland, Robert L. *Tobacco, from the Seed to the Salesroom*. Richmond: William Ellis Jones, 1880.

Ransom, Roger L., and Richard Sutch. *One Kind of Freedom: The Economic Consequences of Emancipation*. 2nd ed. Cambridge: Cambridge University Press, 2001.

Rawick, George, ed. *The American Slave: A Composite Autobiography*. Volume 14, Part 1. Westport, Conn.: Greenwood Press, 1972.

Rice, Dorothy Marie, and Lucille Mabel Walthall Payne. *The Seventeenth Child*. North Haven, Conn.: Linnet Books, 1998.

Roark, James. *Masters without Slaves: Southern Planters in the Civil War and Reconstruction*. New York: W. W. Norton, 1978.

Robert, Joseph, C. *The Tobacco Kingdom: Plantation, Market, and Factory in Virginia and North Carolina, 1800–1860*. Durham, N.C.: Duke University Press, 1938.

Saloutos, Theodore. *Farmer Movements in the South, 1865–1933*. Lincoln: University of Nebraska Press, 1964.

Sanders, Elizabeth. *Roots of Reform: Farmers, Workers, and the American State, 1877–1917*. Chicago: University of Chicago Press, 1999.

Schapsmeier, Edward L., and Frederick H. Schapsmeier. "Farm Policy from FDR to Eisenhower: Southern Democrats and the Politics of Agriculture." *Agricultural History* 53 (January 1979): 352–71.

Scharrer, G. Terry. *A Kind of Fate: Agricultural Change in Virginia, 1861–1920*. Ames: Iowa State University Press, 2000.

Schulman, Michael D., and Barbara A. Newman. "The Survival of the Black Tobacco Farmer: Empirical Results and Policy Dilemmas." *Agriculture and Human Values* 8 (Summer 1991): 46–52.

Schweninger, Loren. *Black Property Owners in the South, 1790–1915*. Urbana: University of Illinois Press, 1990.

Shifflett, Crandall A. *Patronage and Poverty in the Tobacco South: Louisa County, Virginia, 1860–1900*. Knoxville: University of Tennessee Press, 1982.

Shirley, Michael. *From Congregation Town to Industrial City: Culture and Social Change in a Southern Community*. New York: New York University Press, 1994.

Siceloff, John. "Tobacco in Transition." *Southern Exposure* 3, no. 4 (1976): 46–52.

Siegel, Frederick F. *The Roots of Southern Distinctiveness: Tobacco and Society in Danville, Virginia, 1780–1865*. Chapel Hill: University of North Carolina Press, 1987.

Smyth, J.F.D. *A Tour in the United States of America.* Vol. 2. London: G. Robinson, 1784.

Somers, Robert. *The Southern States since the War, 1870–71.* Introduction and index by Malcolm C. McMillen. Tuscaloosa: University of Alabama Press, 1965.

————. *Tobacco: The Outlook in America for 1875.* Richmond: Clemmitt & Jones, 1875.

Spirn, Anne Whitson. *Daring to Look: Dorothea Lange's Photographs and Reports from the Field.* Chicago: University of Chicago Press, 2008.

Spriggs, William Edward. "The Virginia Colored Farmers' Alliance: A Case Study of Race and Class Identity." *The Journal of Negro History* 64 (Summer 1979): 191–204.

Steelman, Lala Carr. *The North Carolina Farmers' Alliance: A Political History.* Greenville: East Carolina University Press, 1985.

Stephenson, Shelby. *Greatest Hits: 1978–2000.* Johnstown, Ohio: Pudding House Publications, 2002.

Striffler, Steve. *Chicken: The Dangerous Transformation of America's Favorite Food.* New Haven, Conn.: Yale University Press, 2005.

Sutherland, J. Gwyn. *The Effects of Tobacco Prices and Allotment Variations on Farm Organization and Incomes, Northern Piedmont Area, North Carolina.* Economic Research Report 9. Raleigh: North Carolina Agricultural Experiment Station, 1969.

Tennis, Joe. *Beach to Bluegrass: Places to Brake on Virginia's Longest Road.* Johnson City, Tenn.: Overmountain Press, 2007.

Tilley, Nannie May. "Agitation against the American Tobacco Company in North Carolina, 1890–1911." *North Carolina Historical Review* 24 (April 1947): 207–23.

————. *The Bright-Tobacco Industry, 1860–1929.* Chapel Hill: University of North Carolina Press, 1948.

Tindall, George Brown. *The Emergence of the New South, 1913–1945.* Baton Rouge: Louisiana State University Press, 1967.

Trelease, Allen W. *White Terror: The Ku Klux Klan Conspiracy and Southern Reconstruction.* Baton Rouge: Louisiana State University Press, 1971.

U.S. Commission on Civil Rights. *Where Mules Outrate Men: Migrant and Seasonal Farmworkers in North Carolina: A Report.* Washington, D.C.: Government Printing Office, 1979.

U.S. Department of Agriculture. *Report of the Commissioner of Agriculture for 1867.* Washington, D.C.: Government Printing Office, 1868.

————. *Tobacco Culture.* Farmers' Bulletin 571. Washington, D.C.: Government Printing Office, 1925.

U.S. Department of Agriculture, Agricultural Research Service. "Effects of Maleic Hydrazide on the Suitability of Tobacco for Cigarette Manufacture." Washington, D.C.: Government Printing Office, 1961. http://legacy.library.ucsf.edu/tid/luj13c00/pdf.

U.S. Department of Agriculture Economic Research Service. *Direct and Contract Hiring of Seasonal Farm Labor.* Statistical Bulletin 478. Washington, D.C.: U.S. Department of Agriculture, 1972.

U.S. Department of Commerce, Bureau of the Census. *Census of Agriculture, 1935: Virginia.* Washington D.C.: Government Printing Office, 1938.

———. *Census of Agriculture: 1945.* Parts 15 and 16. Washington D.C.: Government Printing Office, 1946.

———. *Fourteenth Census of the United States. State Compendium: North Carolina. Statistics of Population, Occupations, Agriculture, Irrigation, Drainage, Manufactures, and Mines and Quarries for the State, County, and Cities.* Washington, D.C.: Government Printing Office, 1924.

———. *Fourteenth Census of the United States. State Compendium: Virginia. Statistics of Population, Occupations, Agriculture, Irrigation, Drainage, Manufactures, and Mines and Quarries for the State, County, and Cities.* Washington, D.C.: Government Printing Office, 1924.

———. *1964 Census of Agriculture.* Parts 24 and 26. Washington D.C.: Government Printing Office, 1967.

———. *1974 Census of Agriculture.* Volume 1. Part 46. Washington D.C.: Government Printing Office, 1977.

U.S. Environmental Protection Agency. *Maleic Hydrazide.* R.E.D. Fact Sheet. June 1994. http://www.epa.gov/oppsrrd1/REDs/factsheets/0381fact.pdf.

U.S. House of Representatives. *Field Hearing on Issues Relating to Migrant and Seasonal Agricultural Workers and Their Employers: Hearing Before the Subcommittee on Workforce Protections of the Committee on Education and Workforce, 12 September 1997.* Washington, D.C.: Government Printing Office, 1997.

———. *Hearings before the Joint Commission to Investigate the Purchase of American-Grown Tobacco, June 24–25, 1914.* Washington, D.C.: Government Printing Office, 1914.

U.S. Senate. *Hearings Before a Subcommittee of the Committee on Agriculture and Forestry, United States Senate, on S. 1219, A Bill to Authorize a System of Acreage-Poundage Allotments for Tobacco.* Washington, D.C.: Government Printing Office, 1957.

———. *Hearings Before the United States Senate Select Committee to Investigate Alleged Outrages in Southern States: Testimony on North Carolina, with Minority Report.* Washington, D.C.: Government Printing Office, 1871.

———. *The Necessity of a Tobacco Quota Buyout: Why It Is Crucial to Rural Communities and the U.S. Tobacco Industry, Hearing Before the Subcommittee on Production and Price Competitiveness of the Committee on Agriculture, Nutrition, and Forestry, 13 April 2004.* Washington, D.C.: Government Printing Office, 2004.

———. *Report of the Committee of the Senate upon the Relations between Labor and Capital and Testimony Taken by the Committee.* Volume IV, *Testimony.* Washington, D.C.: Government Printing Office, 1885.

U.S. Senate, Committee on Privileges and Elections. *Inquiry into Massacre of Colored Men at Danville, Va., and Alleged Election Outrages in Virginia, in 1883.* 48th Cong., 1st sess., 1884. Washington, D.C.: Government Printing Office, 1884.

Vernon, J. J., and M. J. B. Ezekiel, *Causes of Profit or Loss on Virginia Tobacco Farms.*

Virginia Agricultural Experiment Station Bulletin 241. Blacksburg: Virginia Polytechnic Institute, 1925.

Virginia Employment Commission. *Virginia Annual Farm Labor Report: 1964.* Richmond: Virginia Employment Commission, 1965.

———. *Virginia Annual Farm Labor Report: 1969.* Richmond: Virginia Employment Commission, 1970.

———. *Virginia Annual Farm Labor Report: 1970.* Richmond: Virginia Employment Commission, 1971.

———. *Virginia Annual Farm Labor Report: 1972.* Richmond: Virginia Employment Commission, 1973.

———. *Virginia Annual Rural Manpower Report: 1973.* Richmond: Virginia Employment Commission, 1974.

Wadley, Janet K., and Everett S. Lee. "The Disappearance of the Black Farmer." *Phylon* 35 (1974): 276–83.

Waldrep, Christopher. *Night Riders: Defending Community in the Black Patch, 1890–1915.* Durham, N.C.: Duke University Press, 1993.

Wasem, Ruth Ellen, and Geoffrey K. Colliver. *Immigration and Agricultural Guest Workers: Policy, Trends, and Legislative Issues.* Washington, D.C.: Congressional Research Service, 15 February 2001.

Wilson, Emmy, and Claude W. Anderson, "Interview with Nancy Williams." [18 May 1937.] In *Weevils in the Wheat: Interviews with Virginia Ex-Slaves,* edited by Charles L. Perdue Jr., Thomas E. Barden, and Robert K. Phillips, 315–323. Charlottesville: University Press of Virginia, 1976.

Woeste, Victoria Saker. *The Farmer's Benevolent Trust: Law and Agricultural Cooperation in Industrial America.* Chapel Hill: University of North Carolina Press, 1998.

Womach, Jasper, "Tobacco Price Support: An Overview of the Program." Congressional Research Service Report, 2004. http://congressionalresearch.com/95-129/document.php?study=Tobacco+Price+Support+An+Overview+of+the+Program. Accessed 20 February 2014.

Woodman, Harold D. *New South—New Law: The Legal Foundations of Credit and Labor Relations in the Postbellum Agricultural South.* Baton Rouge: Louisiana State University Press, 1995.

Woofter, T. J., Jr. *The Plight of Cigarette Tobacco.* Chapel Hill: University of North Carolina Press, 1931.

Wrather, Stephen E. "Tobacco: The Last Stronghold of the Family Farm." *Tobacco News* 4 (December 1962): 1–4.

Wright, Gavin. *Old South, New South: Revolutions in the Southern Economy since the Civil War.* New York: Basic Books, 1986.

Yeargin, Billy. *Remembering North Carolina Tobacco.* Charleston, S.C.: History Press, 2008.

Yeoman, Barry. "Silence in the Fields." *Mother Jones* 26 (January/February 2001): 40–47.

Index

Page numbers in *italics* refer to illustrations.

Tobacco auctions, 6, 37–42, 42; and children, 39–40, 67; closing of, 110–11; farmers' perceptions, 39–43, 46–47; sales calendar, 45–46; social aspects, 41–42, 42; switch to untied tobacco, 93–94; and women, 39–42, 40, 41

Tobacco bags, 17–18

Tobacco barns, 31

Tobacco buyers, 38, 45–46

Tobacco farming: by African Americans, 2, 5, 10–12, 22, 25, 28–29; by children, 2, 5, 8–9, 22, 24–26, 27, 30, 31, 79–80, 95–96; ecology of, 10, 17, 23–24, 26–27; family labor, 3, 5–6, 8–9, 21, 22–34; mechanization, 6, 80, 82–83, 88–92, 93–95; and memory, 1–2, 22–23, 34; by offshore workers, 81, 97–99; planter ideal, 10–12, 22, 23, 43–44; by prisoners of war, 81; by slaves, 2; wage labor, 12–13, 17–18, 21, 30, 95–96; by women, 5, 8–9, 22, 25, 28–29, 30, 32, 79–80, 95

Tobacco grades, 46–47

Tobacco Growers Information Committee, 106–7

Tobacco hands, 32, 33, 34, 93–94

Tobacco hornworms, 1–2, 26

Tobacco Industry Research Council (TIRC), 106

Tobacco inspection, 37, 48–49, 51

Tobacco Institute, 92, 106–7

Tobacco plantations, 5; breakdown of, 19

Tobacco sleds, 30

Tobacco warehouses, 18, 37–38, 45, 67; Alliance-owned warehouses, 56–57

Topping, 25–26

Transplanting, 24–25

Tri-State Tobacco Growers' Cooperative, 6, 64–69; and African Americans, 66–67; appeals to women and families, 67–68; contract-breaking, 69; difficulty organizing sharecroppers, 66–67; gendered rhetoric of organizers, 65–66; opposition from warehousemen, 69; organizing techniques, 64–65, 67–69; support from Extension Service, 65

Truman, Harry S., 86

Tying. See Stringing

Vance, Zebulon, 54

Vance County, North Carolina, 20, 26, 46, 56

Variety Discount Program, 87–88, 89

Violence: against African American landowners, 20; against laborers, 12; political, 13

Wake County, North Carolina, 54, 78, 96

Warehouse Act (1916), 72

Warren County, North Carolina, 35, 68

Weeks, L. T., 86–87, 89

Wilkins, Elvin, 40

Wilkins, Rosa, 40, 41

Wilson, North Carolina, 105

Winston (Winston-Salem), North Carolina, 18, 57, 78

Woofter, T. J., 43, 45, 46

World War I: and tobacco prices, 35, 63

Worming, 1–2, 22, 25–26

Wrather, Stephen E., 75

Yadkin County, North Carolina, 96

Yeargin, Billy, 23

Yeoman, Barry, 98

EVAN P. BENNETT is associate professor of history at Florida Atlantic University. He is the author of *Tampa Bay: The Story of an Estuary and Its People* and coeditor of *Beyond Forty Acres and a Mule: African American Landowning Families since Reconstruction*.